Bugs and Birds in Origami

Bugs and Birds
in Origami

John Montroll

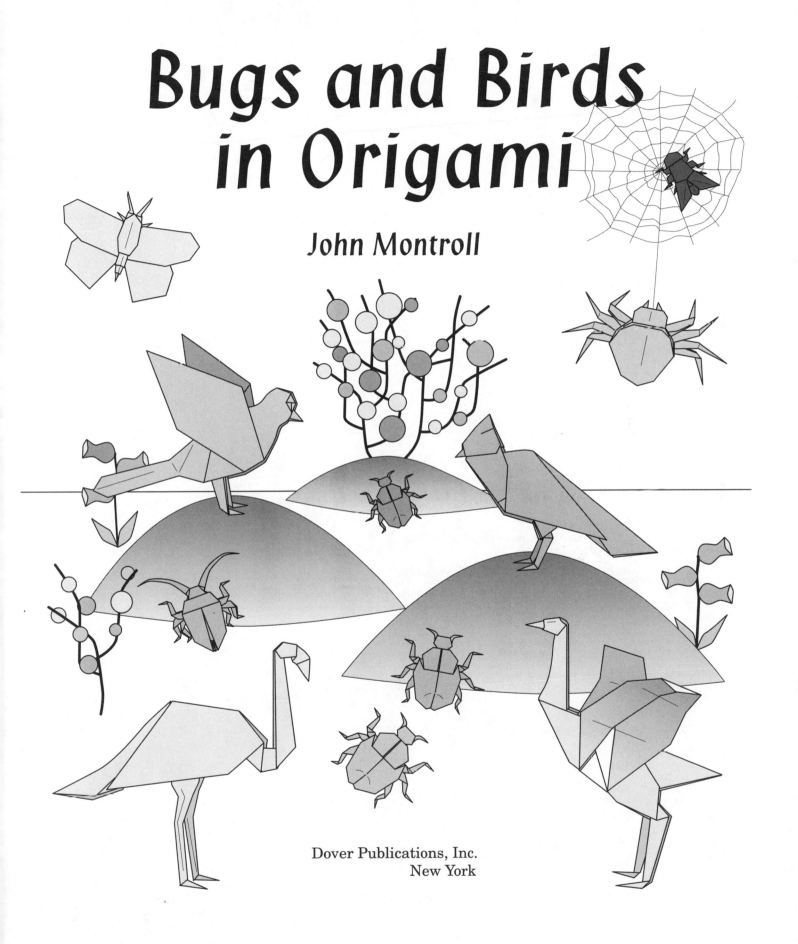

Dover Publications, Inc.
New York

To Sarah and Elliott

Bibliographical Note

This work is first published in 2001 in separate editions by Antroll Publishing Company, Maryland, and Dover Publications, Inc., New York.

Library of Congress Cataloging-in-Publication Data

Montroll, John.
    Bugs and birds in origami / John Montroll.
        p. cm.
    ISBN 0-486-41773-5 (pbk.)
    1. Origami. 2.Insects in art. 3. Birds in art. I. Title.
TT870.M5532 2001
736'.982—dc21

2001028462

Manufactured in the United States of America
    Dover Publications, Inc., 31 East 2nd Street, Mineola, N.Y. 11501

Introduction

Welcome to Bugs and Birds in Origami. Many of the models in this book utilize a new approach to folding, and this collection of winged and many legged creatures will provide hours of enjoyment to folders everywhere.

The birds, including the cardinal, ibis, and turkey, are excellent projects for intermediate and advanced folders, while the bugs, such as the spider, wasp, and butterfly are more complex and challenging models. In my recent books *Bringing Origami to Life* and *Dollar Bill Animals in Origami*, I concentrated on designing animals with seamless closed backs. The development continues in this book in that most of the birds have seamless closed backs.

I have included only models which can be folded from one uncut square. An inexperienced folder should work from the beginning to the end of the book. The difficulty level increases as you progress, and some of the models use techniques from previous ones. It is interesting to see the similarities in some of the bugs and birds as you fold them.

The illustrations conform to the internationally accepted Randlett-Yoshizawa conventions. The colored side of origami paper is represented by the shadings in the diagrams. Origami paper can be found in many hobby shops or purchased by mail from OrigamiUSA, 15 West 77th Street, New York, NY 10024-5192 or from Dover Publications, Inc., 31 East 2nd Street, Mineola, NY 11501. Large sheets are easier to use than small ones. In general, I recommend using colors which match the animal.

Many people helped make this book possible. I wish to give special thanks to Zach Axelrod, Andrew Belton, Robert Bond, Bill Gallagher, Thomas Gallo, Chris Haresign, Ian Hartman, Russell Hill, Andy Plunket, and Peter Young from St. Anselm's Abbey School for the information and descriptions of the animals. Thanks to my editors, Jonathan Vaile and Charley Montroll. Of course, I also thank the many folders who proof-read the diagrams.

John Montroll

Contents

★	Simple
★★	Intermediate
★★★	Complex
★★★★	Very Complex

Goose
★★
page 10

Cardinal
★★
page 12

Crow
★★
page 15

Snipe
★★
page 16

Ibis
★★
page 19

Flamingo
★★
page 22

Ostrich
★★
page 26

Pheasant
★★
page 30

Quetzal
★★
page 33

Pelican
★★
page 36

Turkey
★★
page 40

Woodpecker
★★
page 44

**Goose with Wings
Outstretched**
★★
page 47

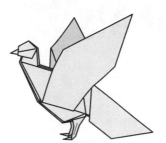

Pigeon
★★
page 50

Hummingbird
★★
page 53

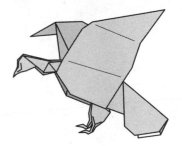

Vulture
★★
page 54

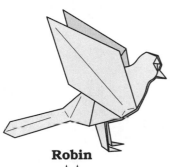

Robin
★★
page 57

Crane
★★
page 59

Parrot
★★
page 63

Stork
★★
page 67

Scavenger Beetle
★★★
page 72

Ladybug
★★★
page 77

Fly
★★★★
page 79

Spider
★★★★
page 85

Wasp
★★★★
page 91

Long-Horned Beetle
★★★★
page 97

Earwig
★★★★
page 103

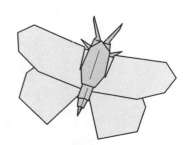

Butterfly
★★★★
page 110

Contents 7

Symbols

Lines

— — — — — — — — Valley fold, fold in front.

—·—··—·—··—·—·— Mountain fold, fold behind.

—————————— Crease line.

·································· X-ray or guide line.

Arrows

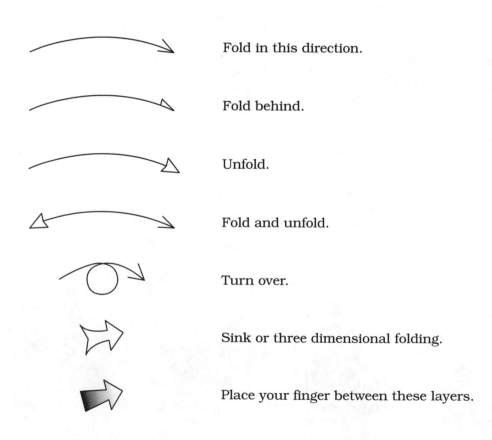

Fold in this direction.

Fold behind.

Unfold.

Fold and unfold.

Turn over.

Sink or three dimensional folding.

Place your finger between these layers.

Practice Bird Heads

Many of the origami birds in this collection use a certain technique to form the heads. The details of this technique are shown here, and you may want to practice folding the head before working on the birds themselves.

1

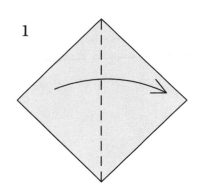

2

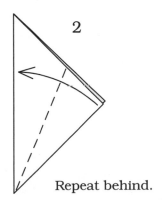

Repeat behind.

3

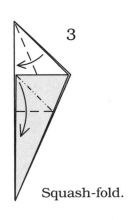

Squash-fold.

4

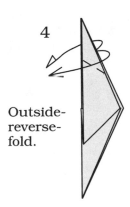

Outside-reverse-fold.

5

Pull out. Repeat behind.

6

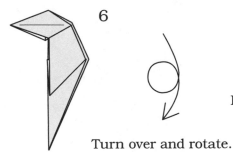

Turn over and rotate.

7

Repeat behind.

8

Repeat steps 4–5. This is the way the bird heads will be diagrammed.

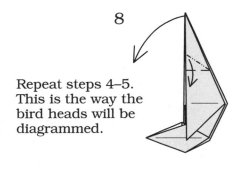

9

Crimp-fold.

10

Crimp-fold the other head.

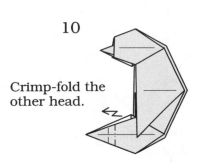

11

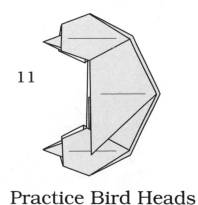

Practice Bird Heads

Goose

Geese are large wild or domestic waterfowl with long necks. They gather in large flocks feeding on grasses, seeds, and aquatic plants in grassy marshes and grain fields. Geese can be quite noisy, and they build nests on the ground from piles of grasses, roots, and sticks.

1

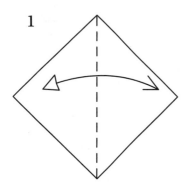

Fold and unfold.

2

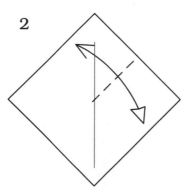

Fold and unfold in the top half.

3

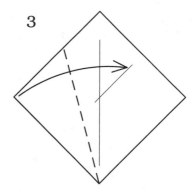

Fold the corner to the line.

4

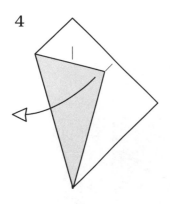

Unfold.

5

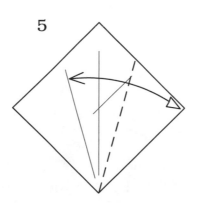

Fold to the crease and unfold.

6

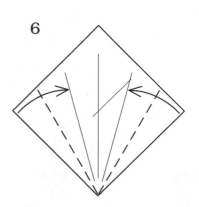

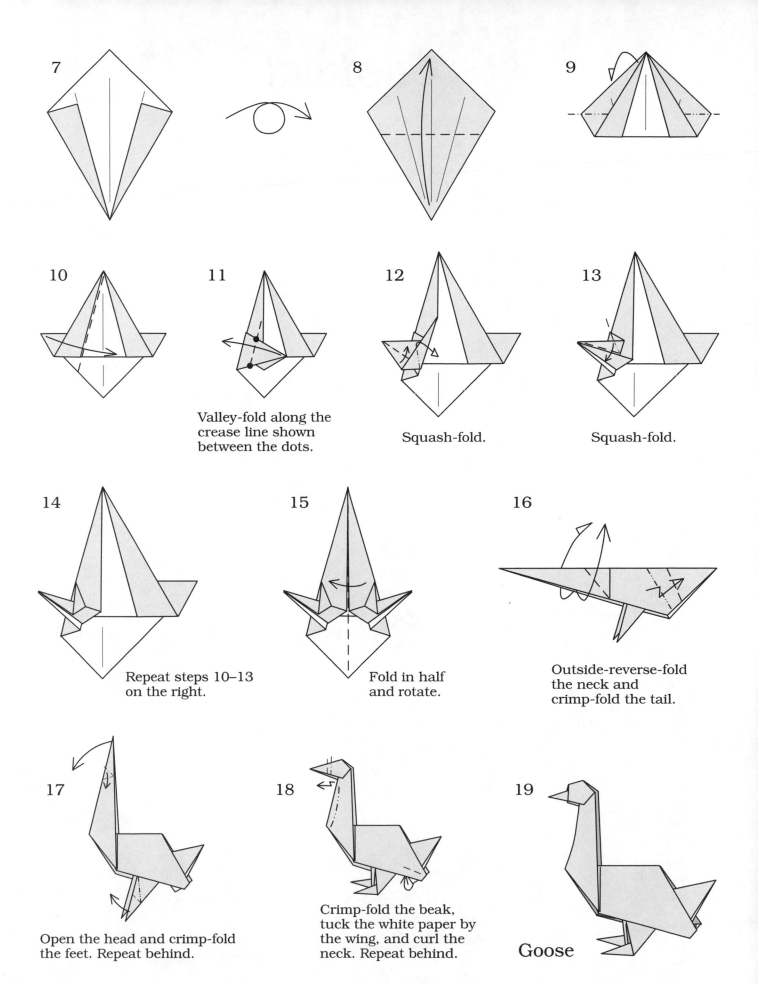

7

8

9

10

11

Valley-fold along the
crease line shown
between the dots.

12

Squash-fold.

13

Squash-fold.

14

Repeat steps 10–13
on the right.

15

Fold in half
and rotate.

16

Outside-reverse-fold
the neck and
crimp-fold the tail.

17

Open the head and crimp-fold
the feet. Repeat behind.

18

Crimp-fold the beak,
tuck the white paper by
the wing, and curl the
neck. Repeat behind.

19

Goose

Cardinal

The cardinal, with its distinguishing crest, is an aggressive and territorial bird. It lives in woodlands, thickets, parks, and gardens. The male cardinal is bright red and the female is brown with a little red on the wings, crest, and bill. With its strong bill, the cardinal can eat hard seeds, along with berries.

1

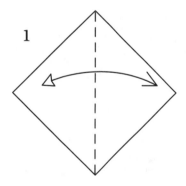

Fold and unfold.

2

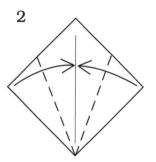

Kite-fold.

3

Unfold.

4

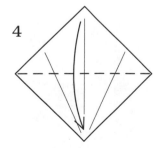

5

Fold and unfold only
one layer on each side.

6

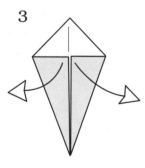

Note the location
of the dots.

7

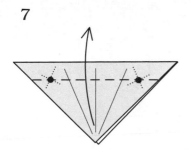

8

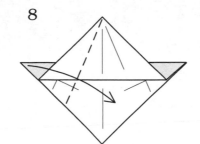

9

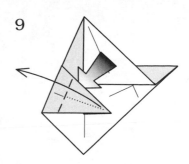

Fold along the crease line
while squash folding
along the x-ray line.

10

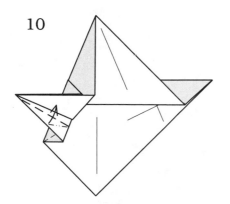

Thin the leg at an
angle of one-third for
this squash fold,

11

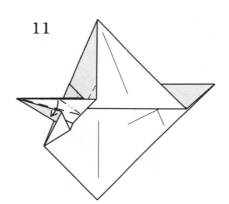

Make two squash folds,
one on the other.

12

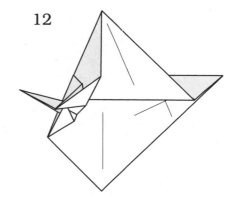

Repeat steps 8–11
on the right.

13

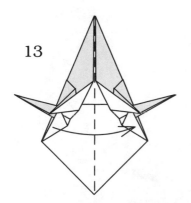

Fold in half
and rotate.

14

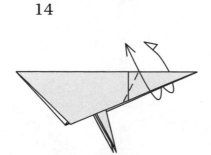

Outside-reverse-fold.

15

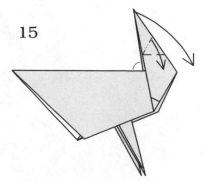

Note that the angle by
the neck is less than 90°.
Open the head.

16

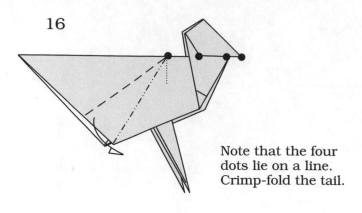

Note that the four dots lie on a line. Crimp-fold the tail.

17

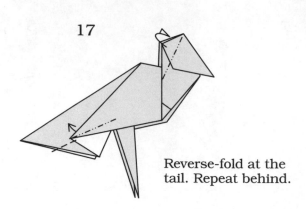

Reverse-fold at the tail. Repeat behind.

18

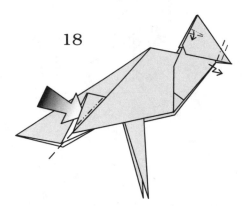

Reverse-fold at the tail, crimp-fold the beak, and make a small crimp at the tuft. Repeat behind.

19

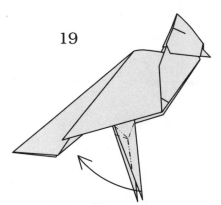

Double-rabbit-ear. Repeat behind.

20

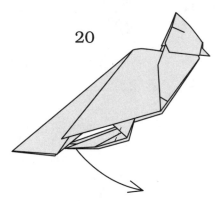

Reverse-fold. Repeat behind.

21

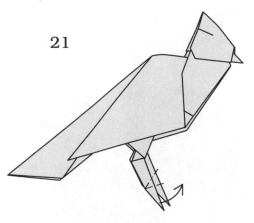

Crimp-fold. Repeat behind.

22

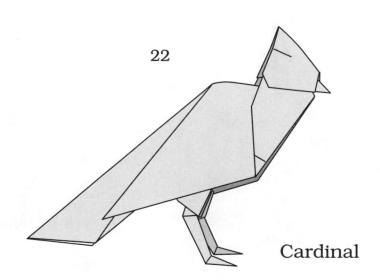

Cardinal

Crow

Crows are noisy, tough, intelligent birds that can be found nearly worldwide in open country, farmland, woodland, and parks. They feed on insects, frogs, small mammals, fruits, grains, and nuts.

6   Crow

1

Begin with step 14 of the cardinal. Outside-reverse-fold.

2

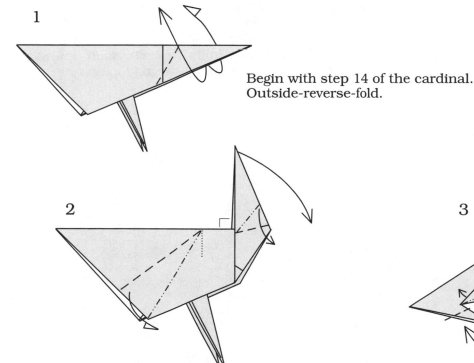

Note that the angle by the neck is 90°. Open the head and crimp-fold the tail. Repeat behind.

3

Fold at an angle of one-third at the head and unfold. Reverse-fold at the tail, double-rabbit-ear the legs. Repeat behind.

4

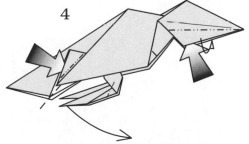

Reverse-fold at the head, tail, and legs. Repeat behind.

5

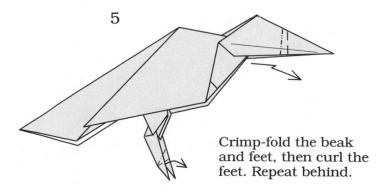

Crimp-fold the beak and feet, then curl the feet. Repeat behind.

Snipe

Snipes are shorebirds that breed on all continents except Australia. They have long, slender bills which are used to probe for worms and grubs in swampy grasslands. They are also known as "woobidah" birds because of the noise made during flight as air rushes around their tail feathers.

1

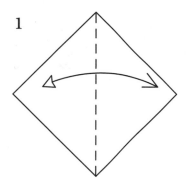

Fold and unfold.

2

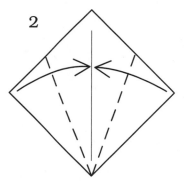

Kite-fold.

3

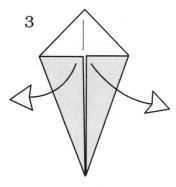

Unfold.

4

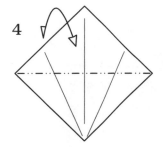

Fold behind
and unfold.

5

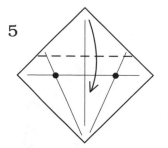

Fold so the edge
meets the dots.

6

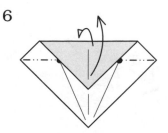

7

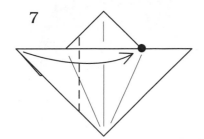

8

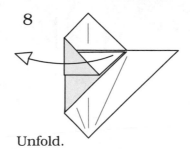

Unfold.

9

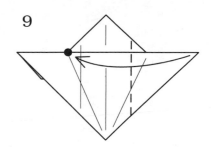

10

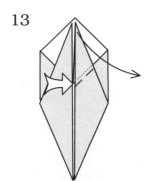

Pivot on the dot.

11

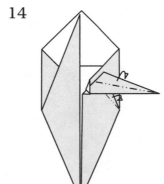

Squash-fold.

12

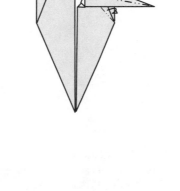

Repeat steps 9–11 on the left.

13

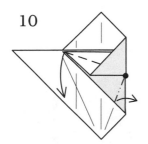

Fold parallel to the dotted line. Squash-fold to form a small triangle.

14

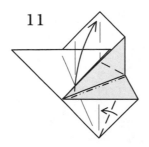

15

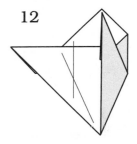

Repeat steps 13–14 on the left.

16

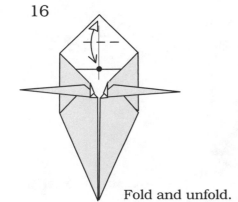

Fold and unfold.

17

18

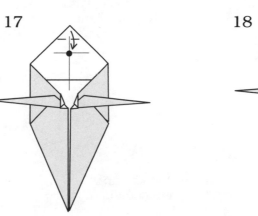

Snipe 17

19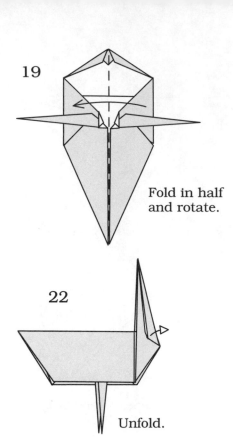

Fold in half
and rotate.

20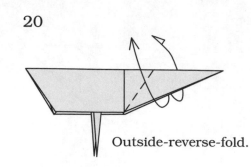

Outside-reverse-fold.

21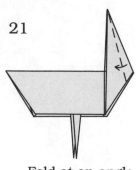

Fold at an angle
of one-third.

22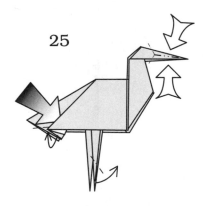

Unfold.

23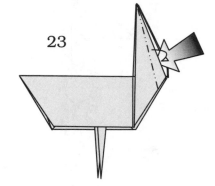

Place your finger into the
upper white layer and
reverse-fold into it. The
layers are not symmetrical.

24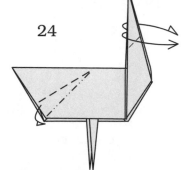

Outside-reverse-fold
the head and
crimp-fold the tail.

25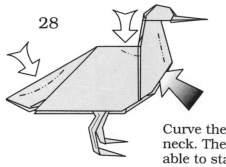

Reverse-fold at the tail,
reverse-fold the feet, and
begin to double-rabbit-ear
the beak. Repeat behind.

26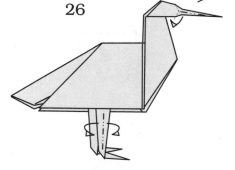

Fold the base of the
beak inside and flatten
the beak. Thin the leg.
Repeat behind.

27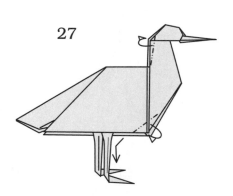

Bend the leg.
Repeat behind.

28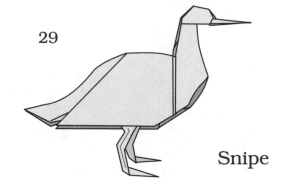

Curve the tail, body, and
neck. The snipe should be
able to stand easily.

29

Snipe

Ibis

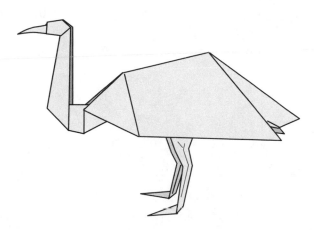

Ibises are long-legged birds that spend much of their time around marshes and swamps. With their long curved bills, they can catch frogs, snakes, insects, and other small animals. Though usually quiet birds, they can make harsh croaking sounds if provoked. These social birds nest and fly in groups. The ibis was considered to be sacred to the ancient Egyptians.

1

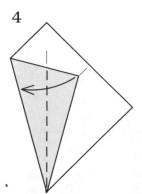

Fold and unfold.

2

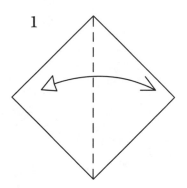

Fold and unfold.

3

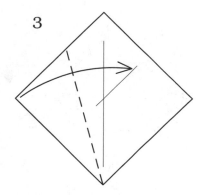

Fold the corner to the line.

4

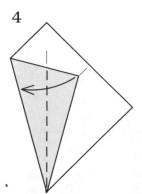

5

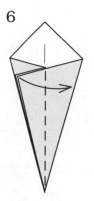

6

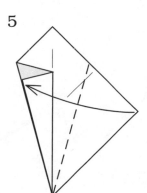

7

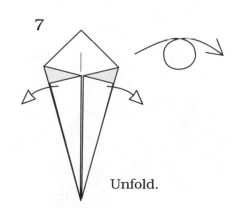

Unfold.

8

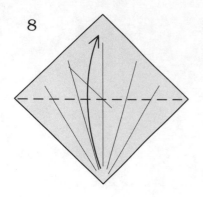

9

Only crease a
little on the left.

10

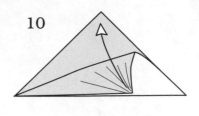

Unfold.

11

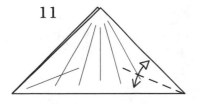

Fold and unfold.

12

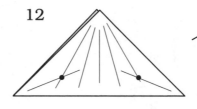

Note the dots.

13

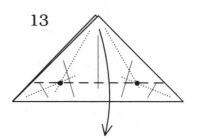

14

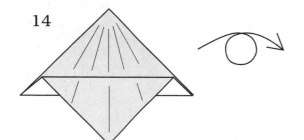

15

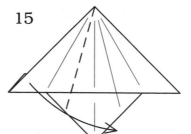

16

Squash-fold.

17

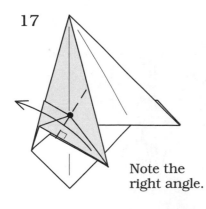

Note the
right angle.

18

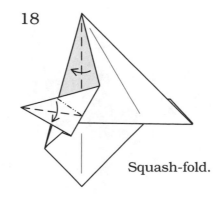

Squash-fold.

19

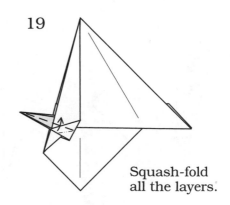

Squash-fold
all the layers.

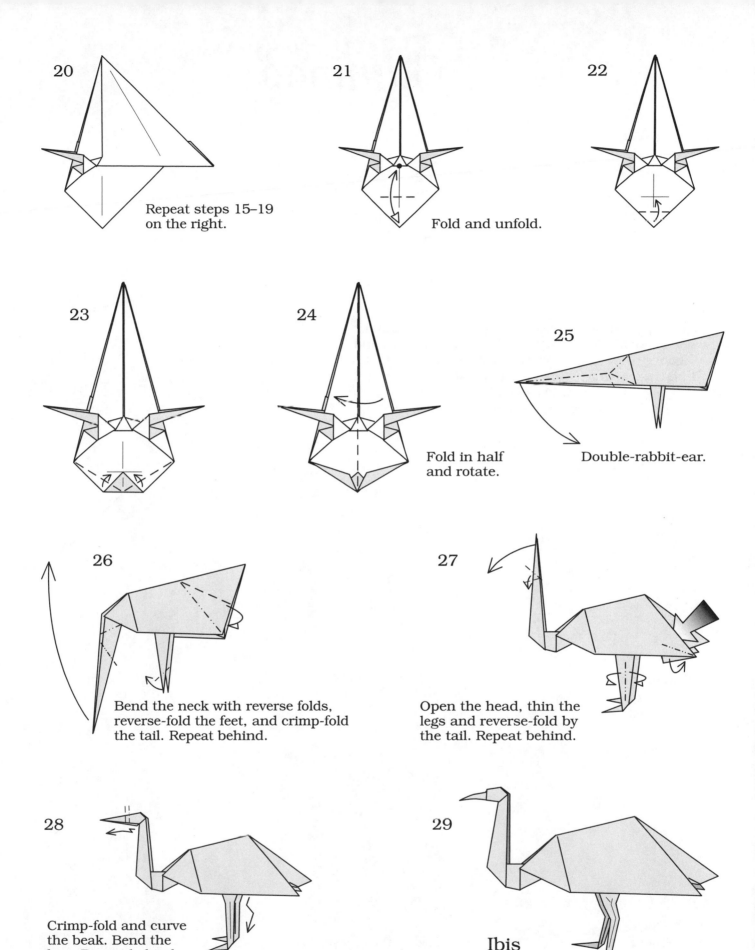

20 Repeat steps 15–19 on the right.

21 Fold and unfold.

22

23

24 Fold in half and rotate.

25 Double-rabbit-ear.

26 Bend the neck with reverse folds, reverse-fold the feet, and crimp-fold the tail. Repeat behind.

27 Open the head, thin the legs and reverse-fold by the tail. Repeat behind.

28 Crimp-fold and curve the beak. Bend the legs. Repeat behind.

29 Ibis

Flamingo

Flamingos are tall birds with long slender legs and necks, and large curved beaks. Living by lakes and lagoons, they stand in shallow water dipping their bills into the water to catch fish, mollusks, crustaceans, insects, and plants. These pink birds often fly at sunrise and sunset, and are also good swimmers.

1

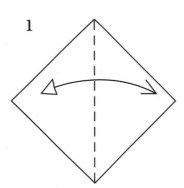

Fold and unfold.

2

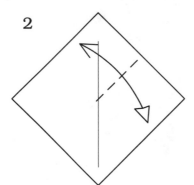

Fold and unfold in the top half.

3

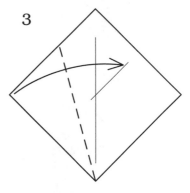

Fold the corner to the line.

4

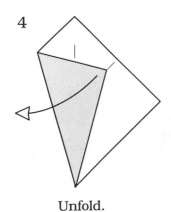

Unfold.

5

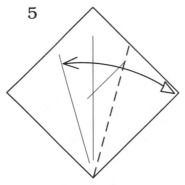

Fold to the crease and unfold.

6

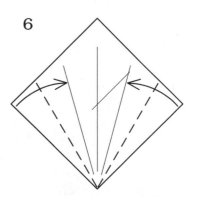

7

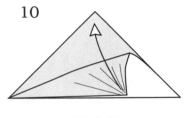

8

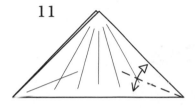

9

Only crease a
little on the left.

10

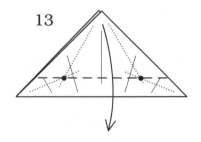

Unfold.

11

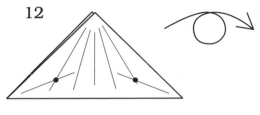

Fold and unfold.

12

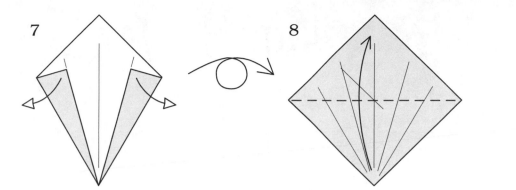

Note the dots.

13

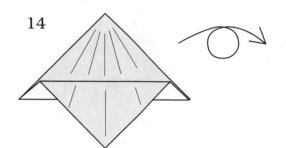

14

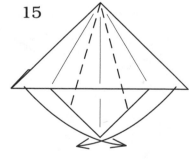

15

16

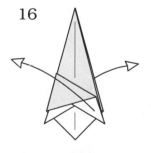

Unfold.

17

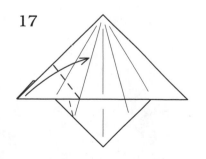

Squash-fold.

18

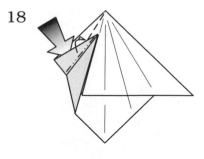

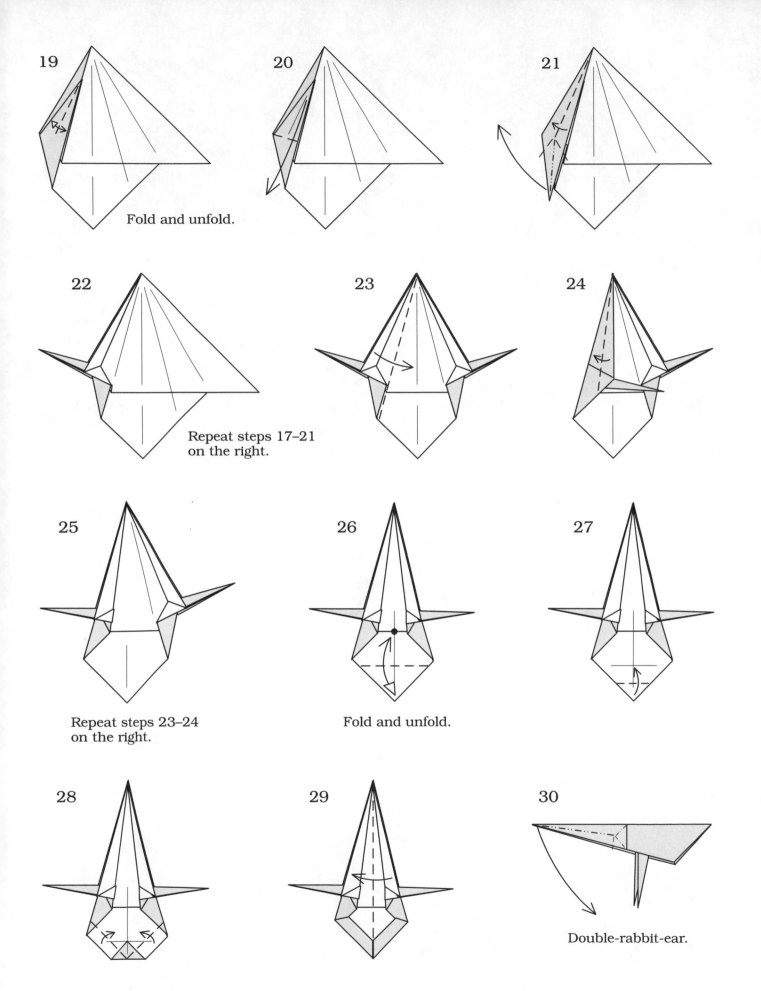

19

20 Fold and unfold.

21

22 Repeat steps 17–21 on the right.

23

24

25 Repeat steps 23–24 on the right.

26 Fold and unfold.

27

28

29

30 Double-rabbit-ear.

31

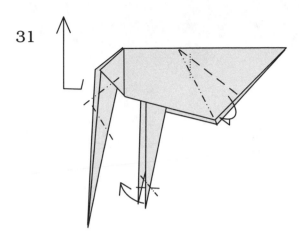

Bend the neck with reverse folds,
reverse-fold the feet, and
crimp-fold the tail. Repeat behind.

32

Open the head and reverse-fold
by the tail. Repeat behind.

33

Pull out to form the beak.
Thin the legs. Repeat behind.

34

Crimp-fold the beak,
curve the tail, and bend
the legs. Repeat behind.

35

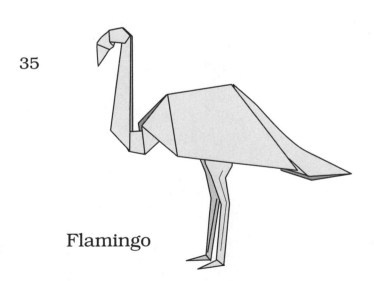

Flamingo

Ostrich

At 8 feet tall and weighing over 300 pounds, the ostrich is the largest bird in the world. Though unable to fly, it can run faster than any two-legged creature. Found in the grasslands of Africa, ostriches wander in small groups in search of food. They feed on plants, berries, seeds, fruits, insects, and small reptiles.

1

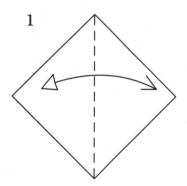

Fold and unfold.

2

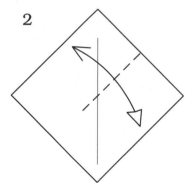

Fold and unfold.

3

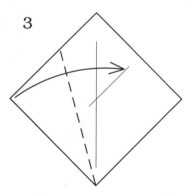

Fold the corner to the line.

4

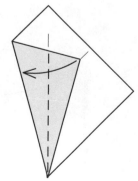

5

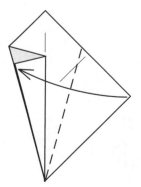

6

7

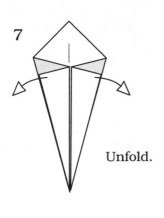

Unfold.

8

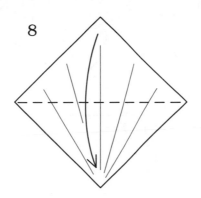

9

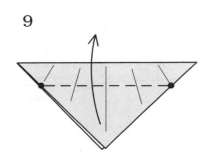

10

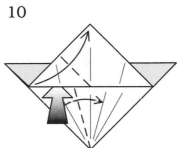

Squash-fold.

11

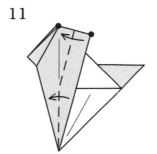

12

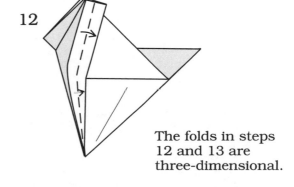

The folds in steps 12 and 13 are three-dimensional.

13

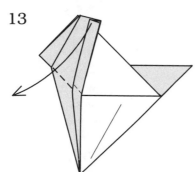

14

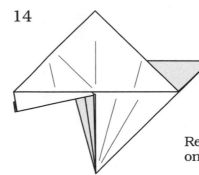

Repeat steps 10–13 on the right.

15

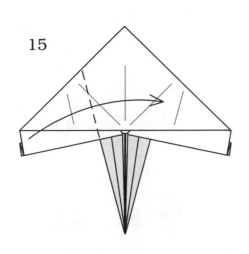

16

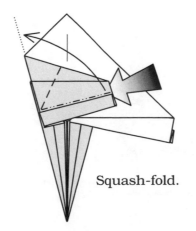

Squash-fold.

17

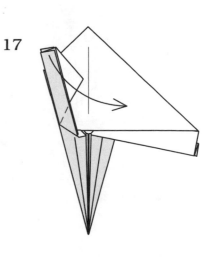

Ostrich 27

18

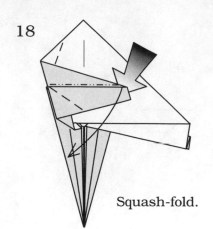

Squash-fold.

19

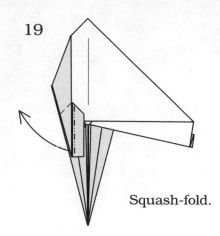

Squash-fold.

20

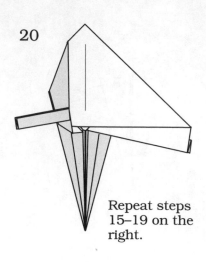

Repeat steps 15–19 on the right.

21

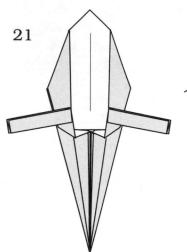

22

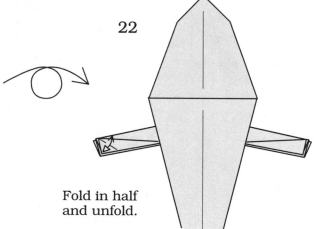

Fold in half and unfold.

23

Two reverse folds.

24

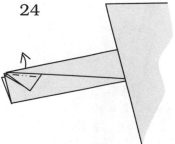

Reverse-fold.

25

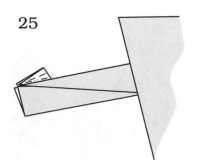

Two reverse folds.

26

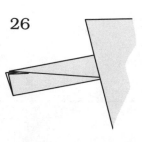

Repeat steps 22–25 behind and on the right to form the remaining toes.

27

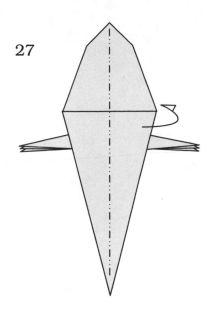

28

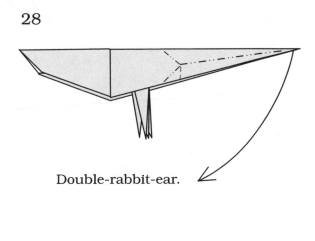

Double-rabbit-ear.

29

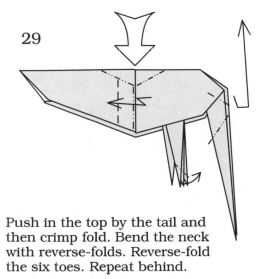

Push in the top by the tail and then crimp fold. Bend the neck with reverse-folds. Reverse-fold the six toes. Repeat behind.

30

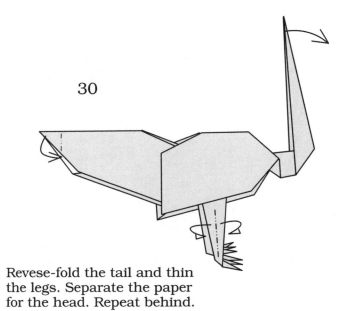

Revese-fold the tail and thin the legs. Separate the paper for the head. Repeat behind.

31

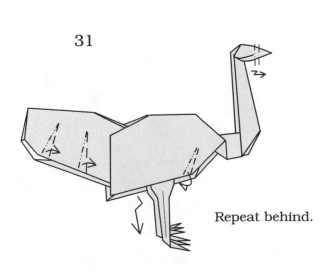

Repeat behind.

32

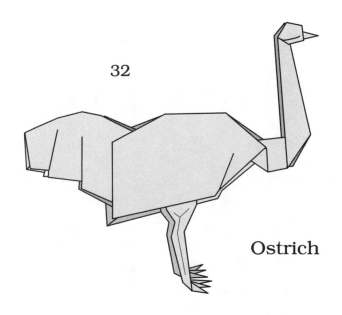

Ostrich

Pheasant

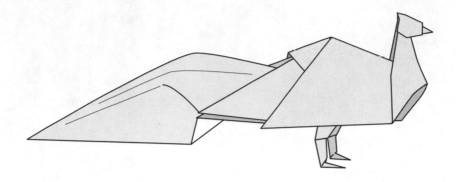

Pheasants are long-tailed bird of open woodlands and fields, where they feed in small flocks. They were originally found between China and Malaysia, but have since been naturalized elsewhere, including Europe and the United States. Many pheasants are prized as ornamental birds in zoos and private collections.

1

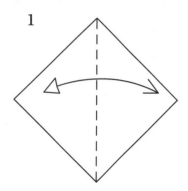

Fold and unfold.

2

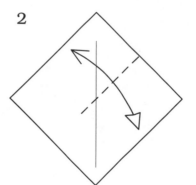

Fold and unfold.

3

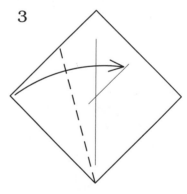

Fold the corner to the line. Rotate.

4

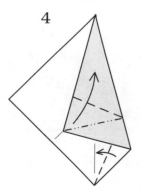

Squash-fold.

5

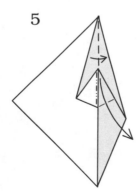

Squash-fold.

6

Squash-fold.

7

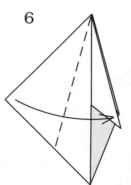

Squash-fold.

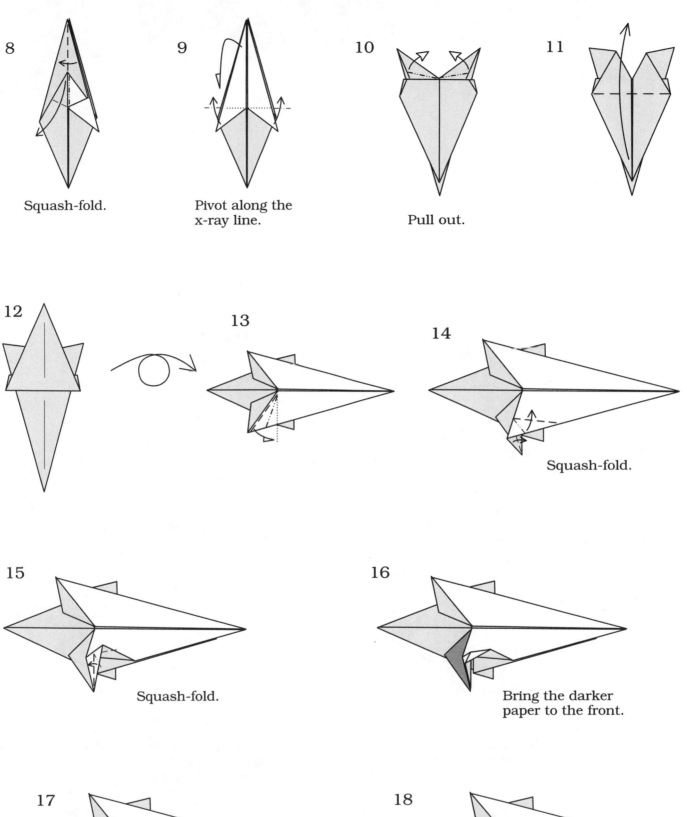

8
Squash-fold.

9
Pivot along the
x-ray line.

10
Pull out.

11

12

13

14
Squash-fold.

15
Squash-fold.

16
Bring the darker
paper to the front.

17
Reverse-fold.

18
Repeat steps
13–17 on the top.

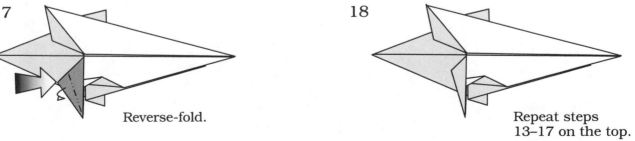

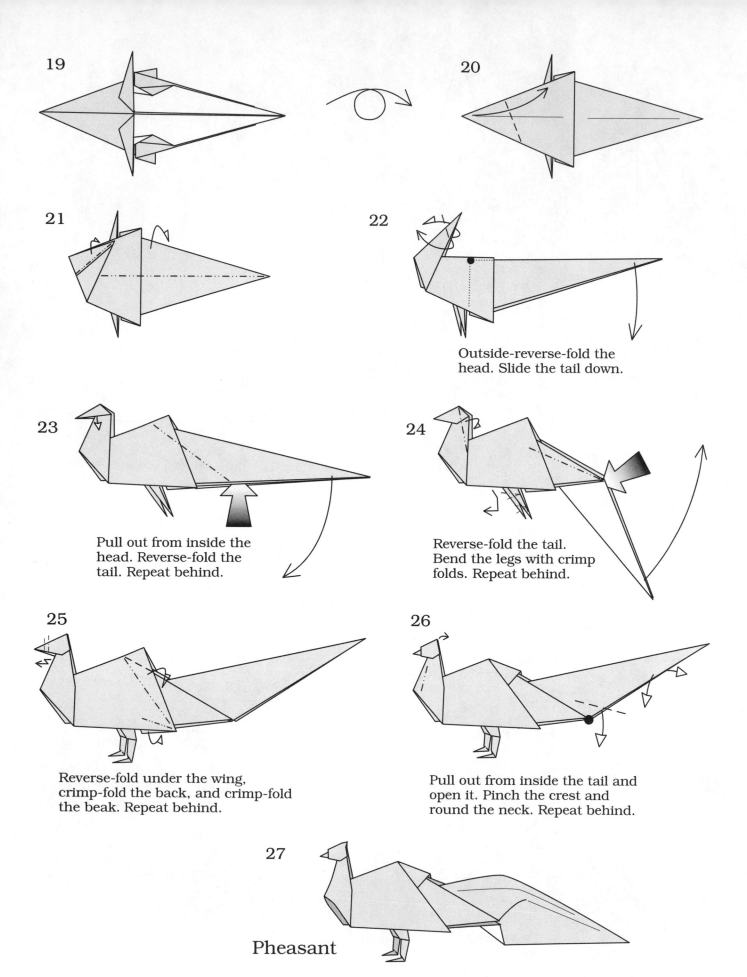

19

20

21

22

Outside-reverse-fold the
head. Slide the tail down.

23

Pull out from inside the
head. Reverse-fold the
tail. Repeat behind.

24

Reverse-fold the tail.
Bend the legs with crimp
folds. Repeat behind.

25

Reverse-fold under the wing,
crimp-fold the back, and crimp-fold
the beak. Repeat behind.

26

Pull out from inside the tail and
open it. Pinch the crest and
round the neck. Repeat behind.

27

Pheasant

Quetzal

A wondrous bird living in Central and South American rain forests, the Quetzal has long been admired for its beauty. Long blue-green plumes cover the bird's tail, which also shows white in flight. The quetzal has a rounded, hairlike crest and a gold-green breast. Its back is blue, its mantle is curly and gold tinged, and its belly is red. It was sacred to the ancient Mayans, who adorned themselves with its long feathers. Today, it is the national bird of Guatemala, whose currency is also the quetzal.

1

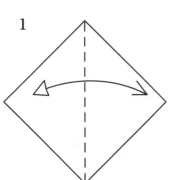

Fold and unfold.

2

Fold and unfold.

3

Fold the corner to the line. Rotate.

4

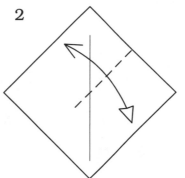

Squash-fold.

5

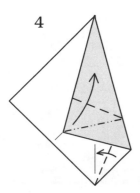

Squash-fold.

6

Squash-fold.

7

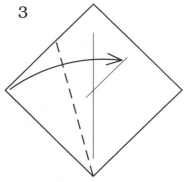

Squash-fold.

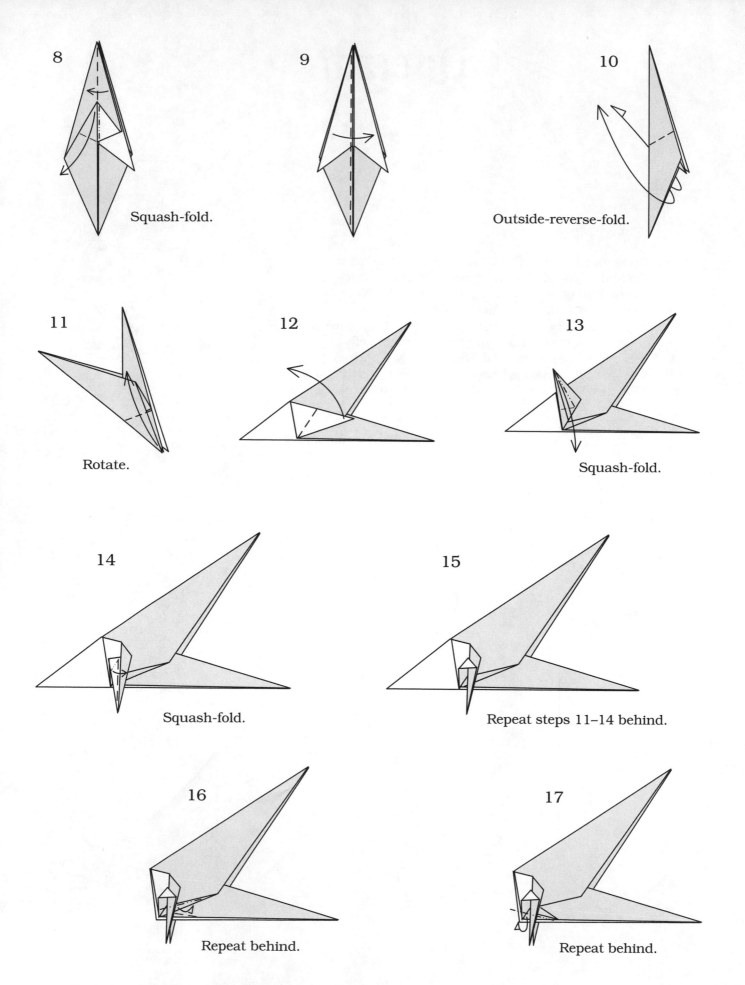

8   Squash-fold.

9

10   Outside-reverse-fold.

11   Rotate.

12

13   Squash-fold.

14   Squash-fold.

15   Repeat steps 11–14 behind.

16   Repeat behind.

17   Repeat behind.

18

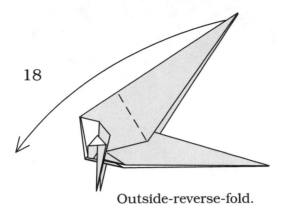

Outside-reverse-fold.

19

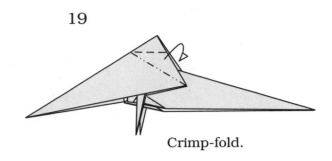

Crimp-fold.

20

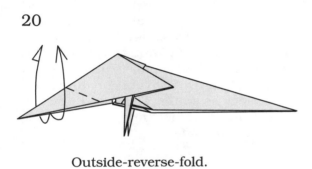

Outside-reverse-fold.

21

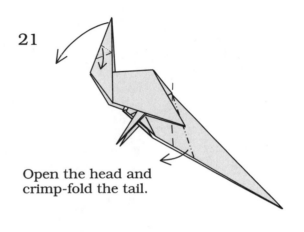

Open the head and
crimp-fold the tail.

22

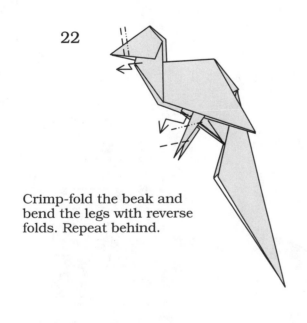

Crimp-fold the beak and
bend the legs with reverse
folds. Repeat behind.

23

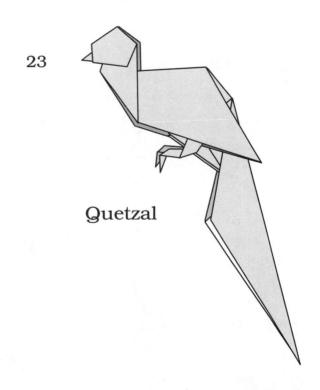

Quetzal

Quetzal 35

Pelican

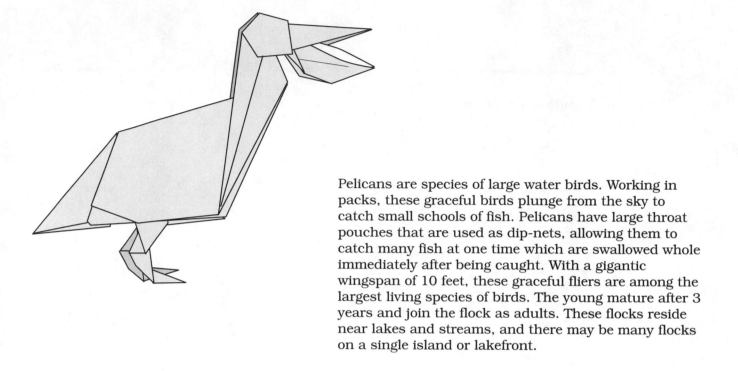

Pelicans are species of large water birds. Working in packs, these graceful birds plunge from the sky to catch small schools of fish. Pelicans have large throat pouches that are used as dip-nets, allowing them to catch many fish at one time which are swallowed whole immediately after being caught. With a gigantic wingspan of 10 feet, these graceful fliers are among the largest living species of birds. The young mature after 3 years and join the flock as adults. These flocks reside near lakes and streams, and there may be many flocks on a single island or lakefront.

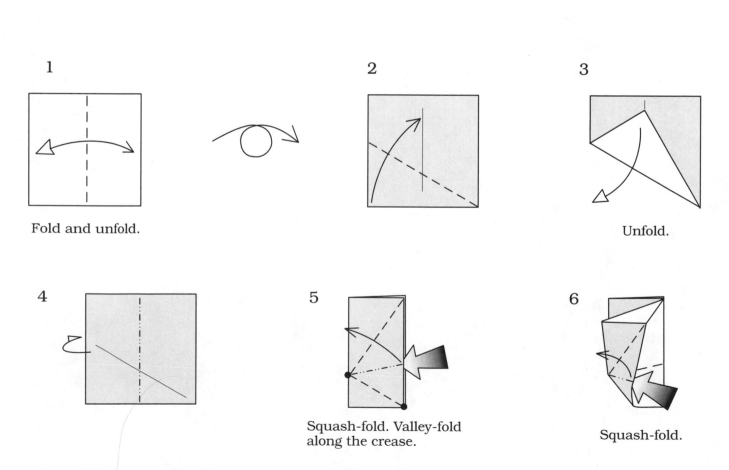

1

Fold and unfold.

2

3

Unfold.

4

5

Squash-fold. Valley-fold along the crease.

6

Squash-fold.

7

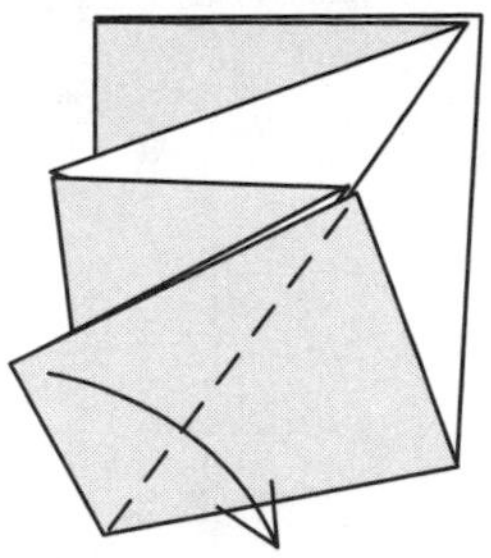

8

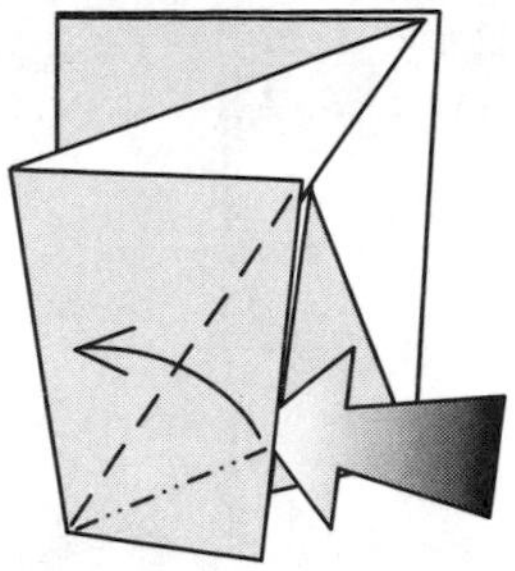

Squash-fold.

9

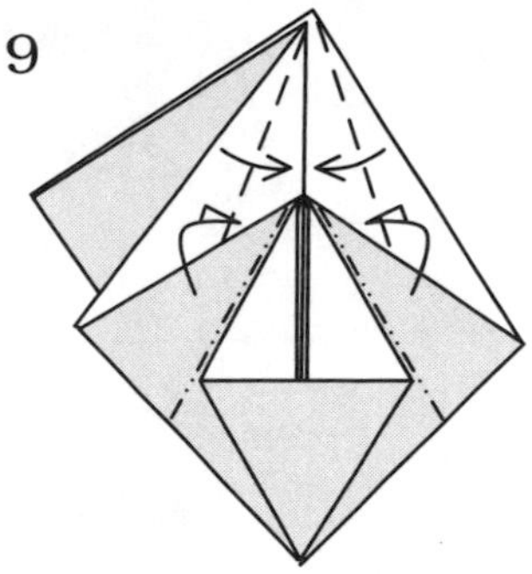

10

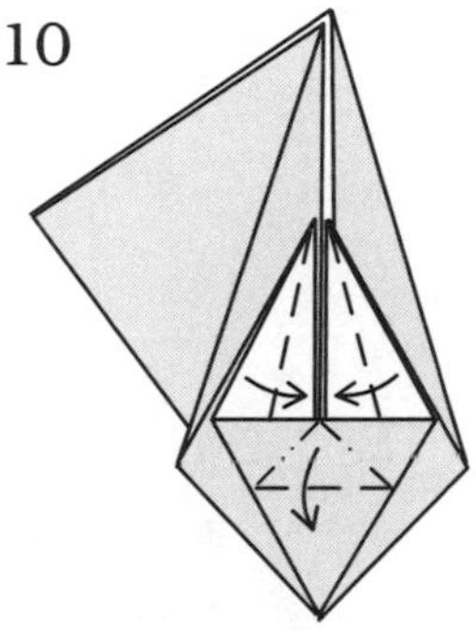

Petal-fold.

11

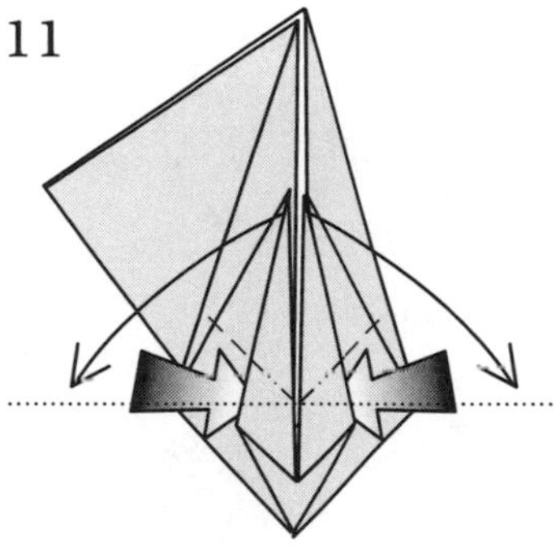

Reverse folds.

12

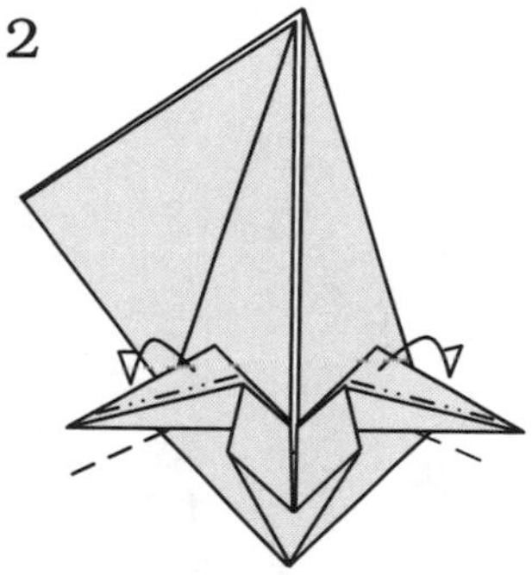

Reverse folds.

13

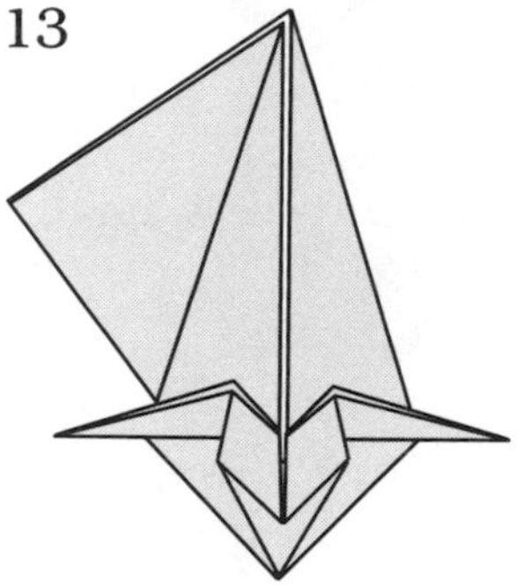

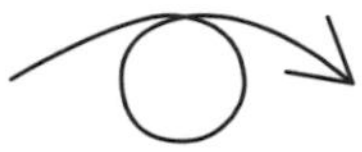

14

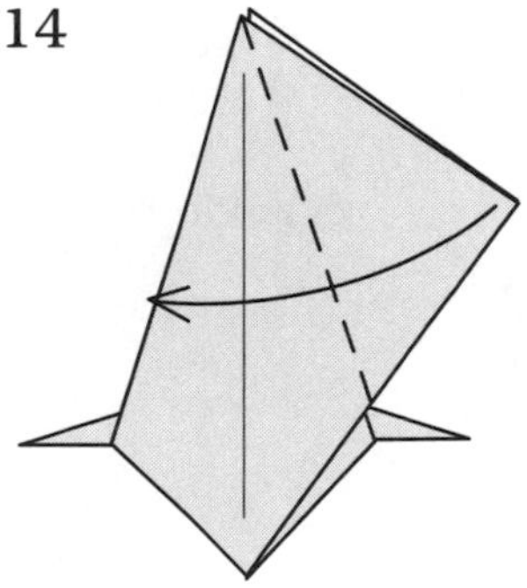

15

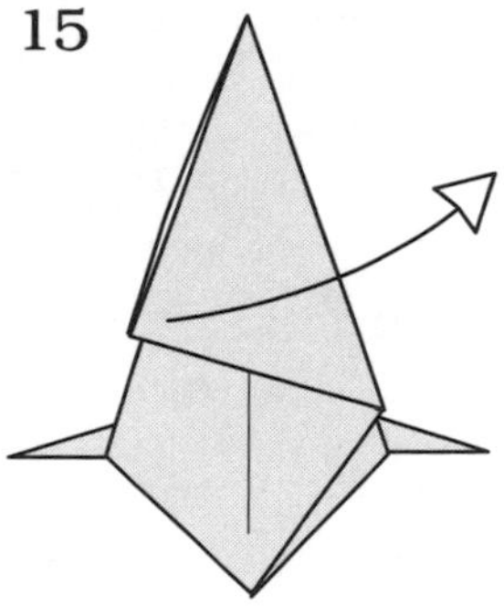

Unfold.

16

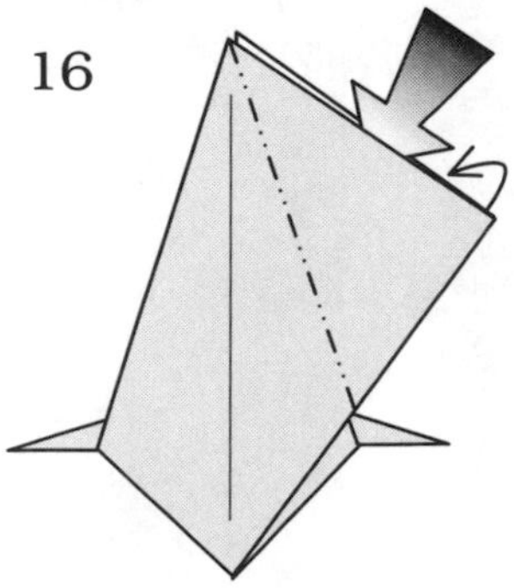

Reverse-fold.

17

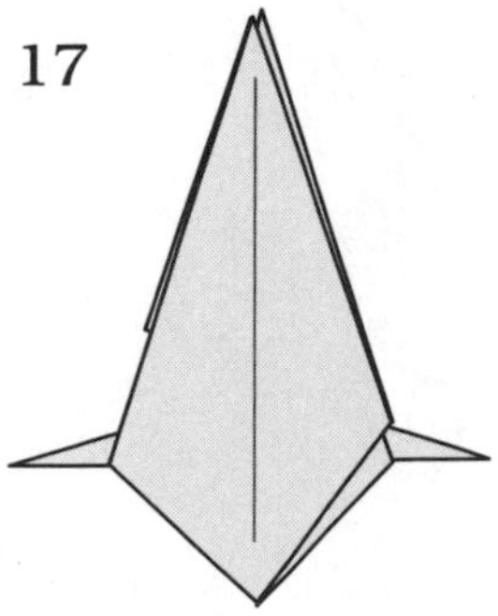

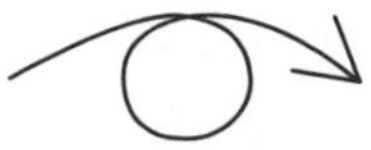

18

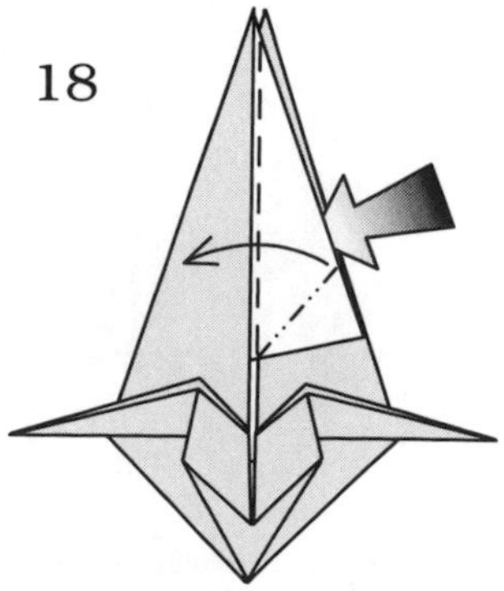

Squash-fold.

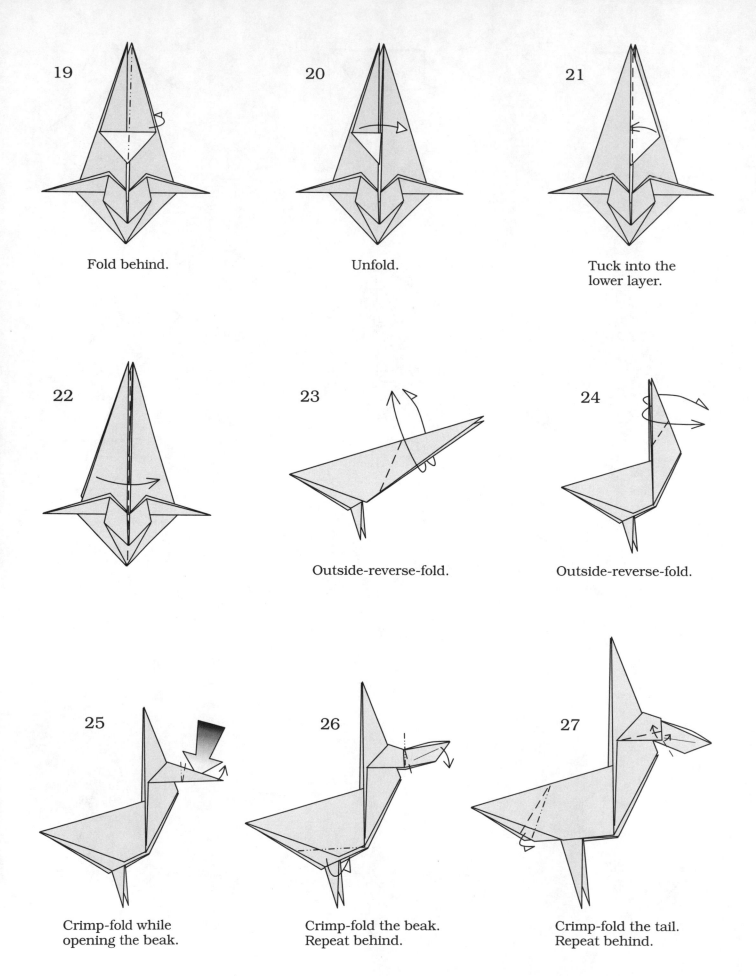

19 Fold behind.

20 Unfold.

21 Tuck into the lower layer.

22

23 Outside-reverse-fold.

24 Outside-reverse-fold.

25 Crimp-fold while opening the beak.

26 Crimp-fold the beak. Repeat behind.

27 Crimp-fold the tail. Repeat behind.

28

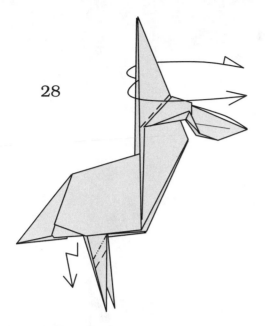

Outside-reverse-fold the
head and crimp-fold the
legs. Repeat behind.

29

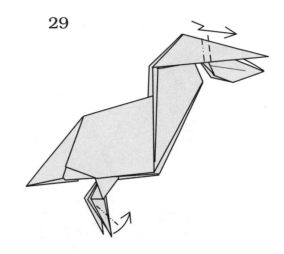

Crimp-fold the beak
and reverse-fold the
feet. Repeat behind.

30

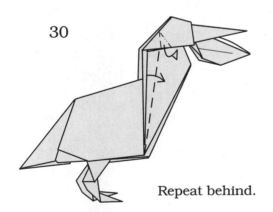

Repeat behind.

31

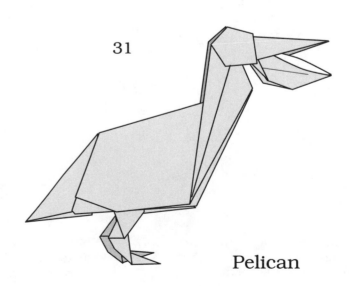

Pelican

Turkey

Turkeys are the largest game birds in North America. They eat nuts, acorns, fruit, insects, and small reptiles. They also swallow stones and pebbles to crush the nuts and acorns in their gizzard. They are strong fliers for short distances.

1

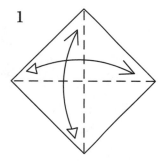

Fold and unfold.

2

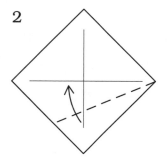

Crease lightly.

3

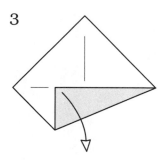

Unfold.

4

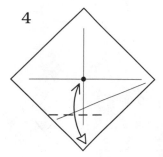

Fold up to the center and unfold. Crease lightly and only on the left side.

5

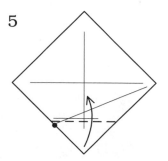

Fold up so the dot meets the line above it.

6

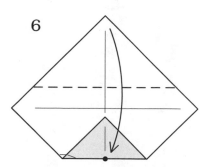

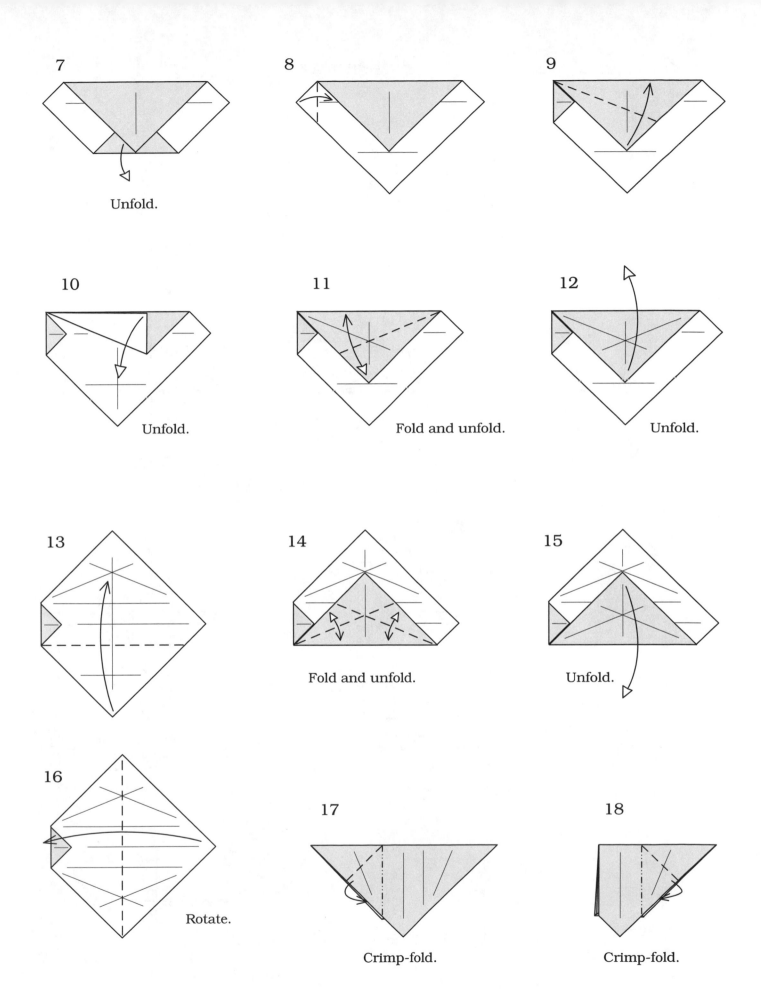

7

Unfold.

8

9

10

Unfold.

11

Fold and unfold.

12

Unfold.

13

14

Fold and unfold.

15

Unfold.

16

Rotate.

17

Crimp-fold.

18

Crimp-fold.

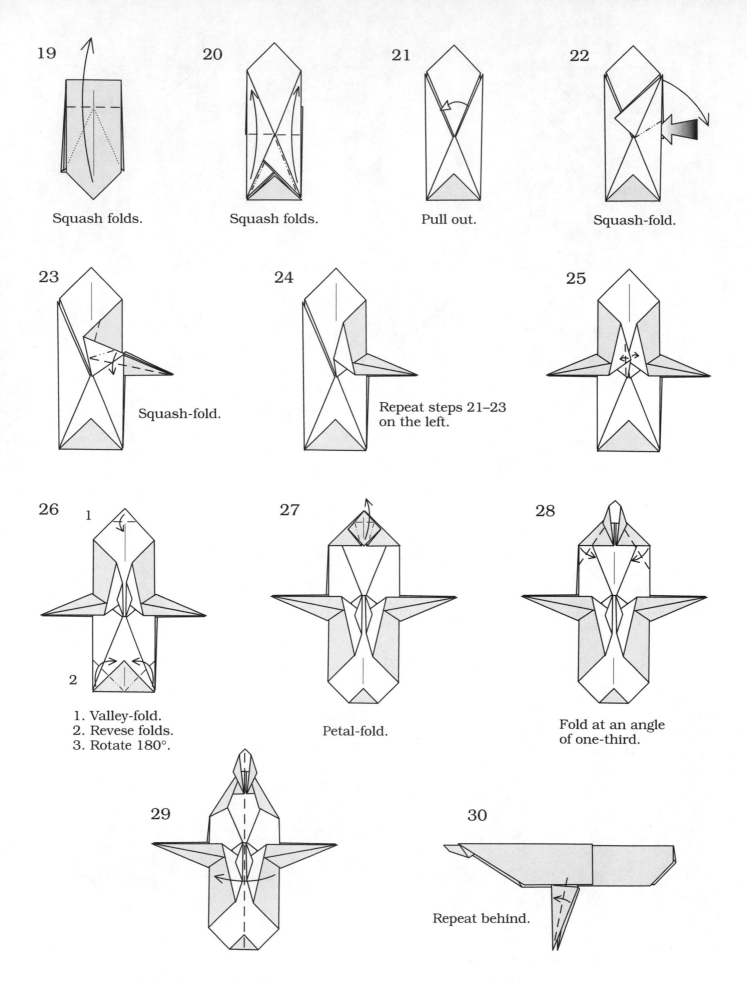

19 Squash folds.

20 Squash folds.

21 Pull out.

22 Squash-fold.

23 Squash-fold.

24 Repeat steps 21–23 on the left.

25

26
1
2
1. Valley-fold.
2. Revese folds.
3. Rotate 180°.

27 Petal-fold.

28 Fold at an angle of one-third.

29

30 Repeat behind.

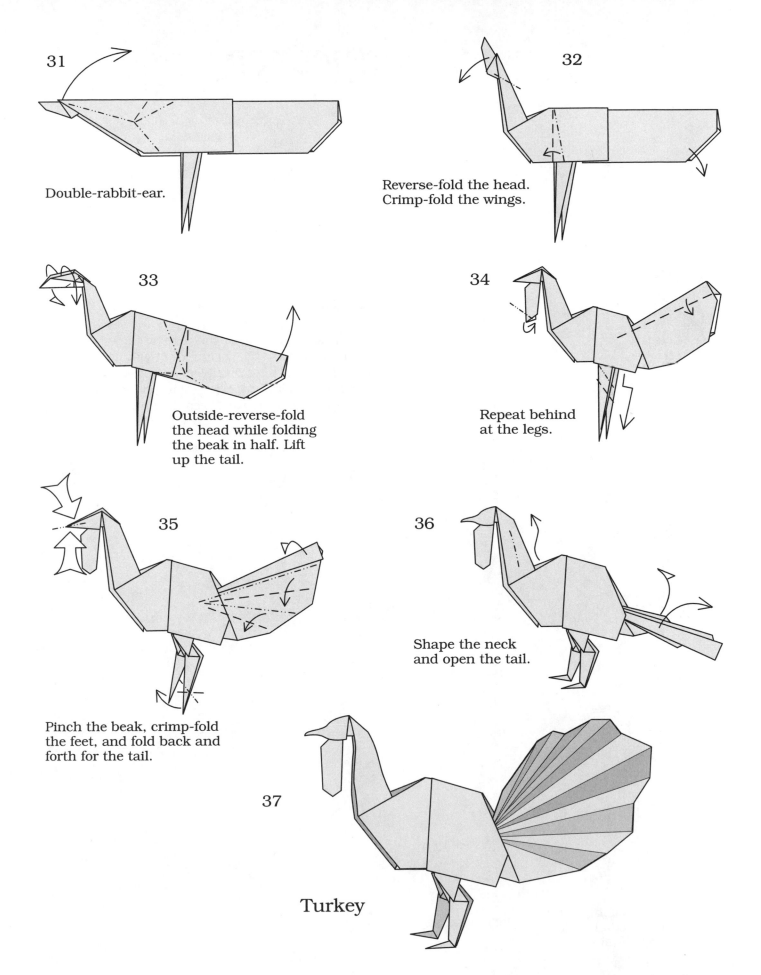

31 Double-rabbit-ear.

32 Reverse-fold the head. Crimp-fold the wings.

33 Outside-reverse-fold the head while folding the beak in half. Lift up the tail.

34 Repeat behind at the legs.

35 Pinch the beak, crimp-fold the feet, and fold back and forth for the tail.

36 Shape the neck and open the tail.

37 Turkey

Woodpecker

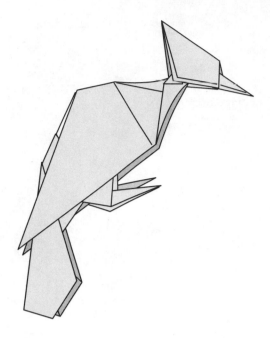

Woodpeckers are adapted for climbing trees and drilling holes in tree trunks with their sharp beaks. They can be heard throughout the year by the rat-a-tat of their drilling. They cling tightly to tree trunks with their sharply clawed feet with toes going both forward and backward. With their long tongues, they can pick insects from the holes they have bored.

1

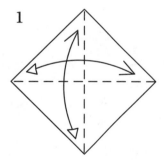

Fold and unfold.

2

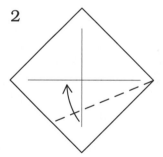

Crease lightly.

3

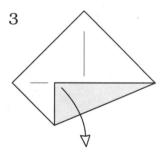

Unfold.

4

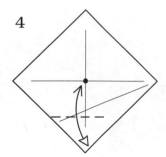

Fold up to the center and unfold. Crease lightly and only on the left side.

5

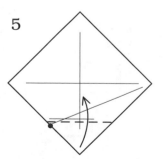

Fold up so the dot meets the line above it.

6

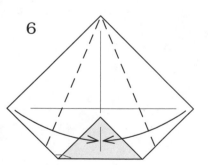

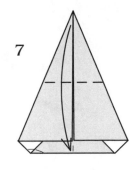

7

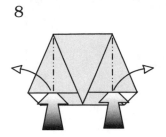

8

Pull out.

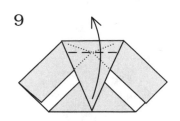

9

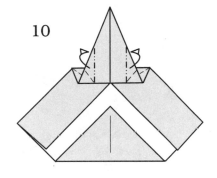

10

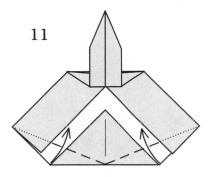

11

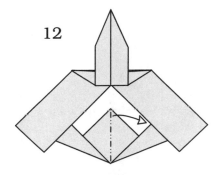

12

Pull out.

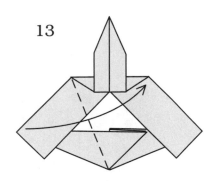

13

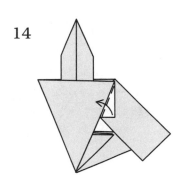

14

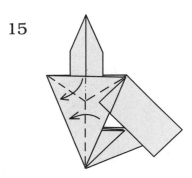

15

Rabbit-ear.

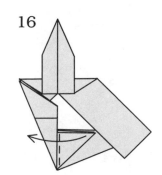

16

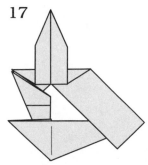

17

Repeat steps 13–15
on the right.

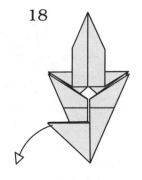

18

Pull out.

19

Squash-fold.

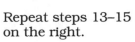

Woodpecker 45

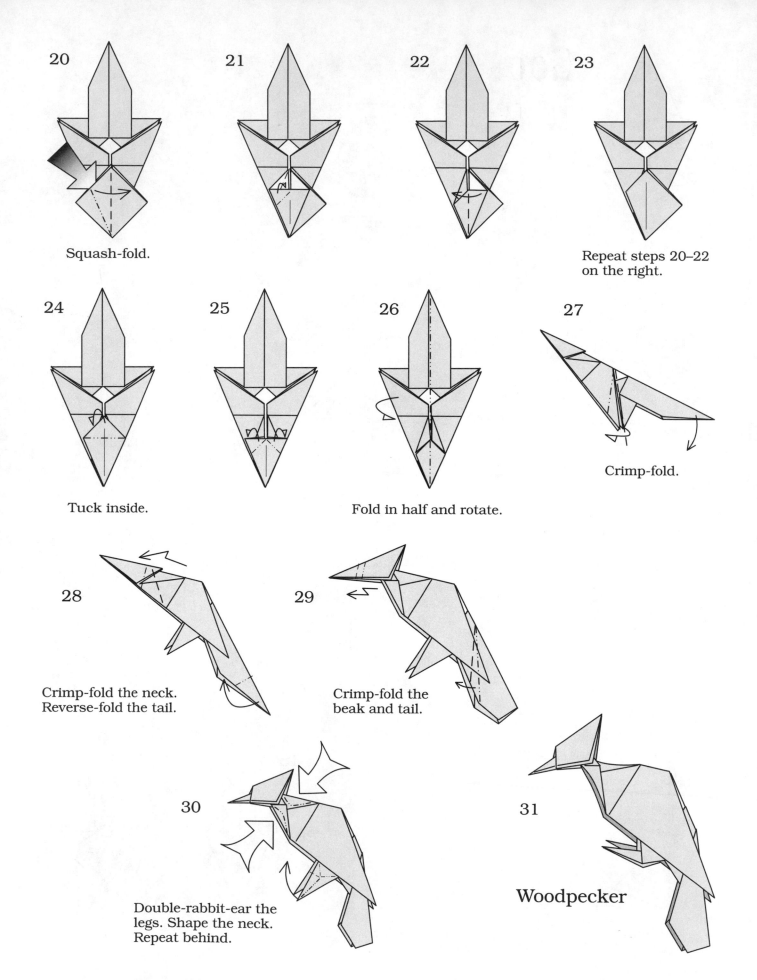

20

Squash-fold.

21

22

23

Repeat steps 20–22
on the right.

24

Tuck inside.

25

26

Fold in half and rotate.

27

Crimp-fold.

28

Crimp-fold the neck.
Reverse-fold the tail.

29

Crimp-fold the
beak and tail.

30

Double-rabbit-ear the
legs. Shape the neck.
Repeat behind.

31

Woodpecker

Goose with Wings Outstretched

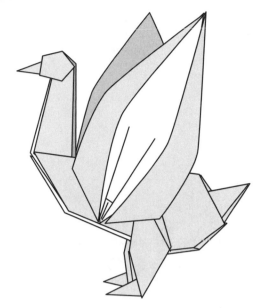

By putting together a collection of origami birds, I ran into the following dilemma; whether a bird is standing with wings folded, outstretched, in flight, or in any other position, the folding patterns would be quite different. I have chosen to represent most of these birds in one position. For the goose and robin I show two positions, with wings down and with wings outstretched. Though the folding for the geese is quite different, I used some similar structures in obtaining the shape of the body, neck, feet, and tail.

1

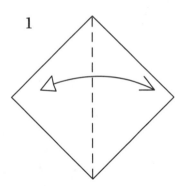

Fold and unfold.

2

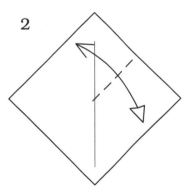

Fold and unfold
in the top half.

3

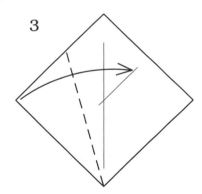

Fold the corner
to the line.

4

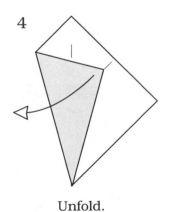

Unfold.

5

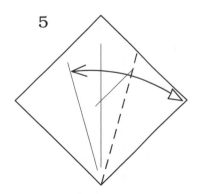

Fold to the crease
and unfold.

6

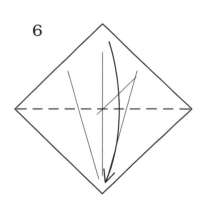

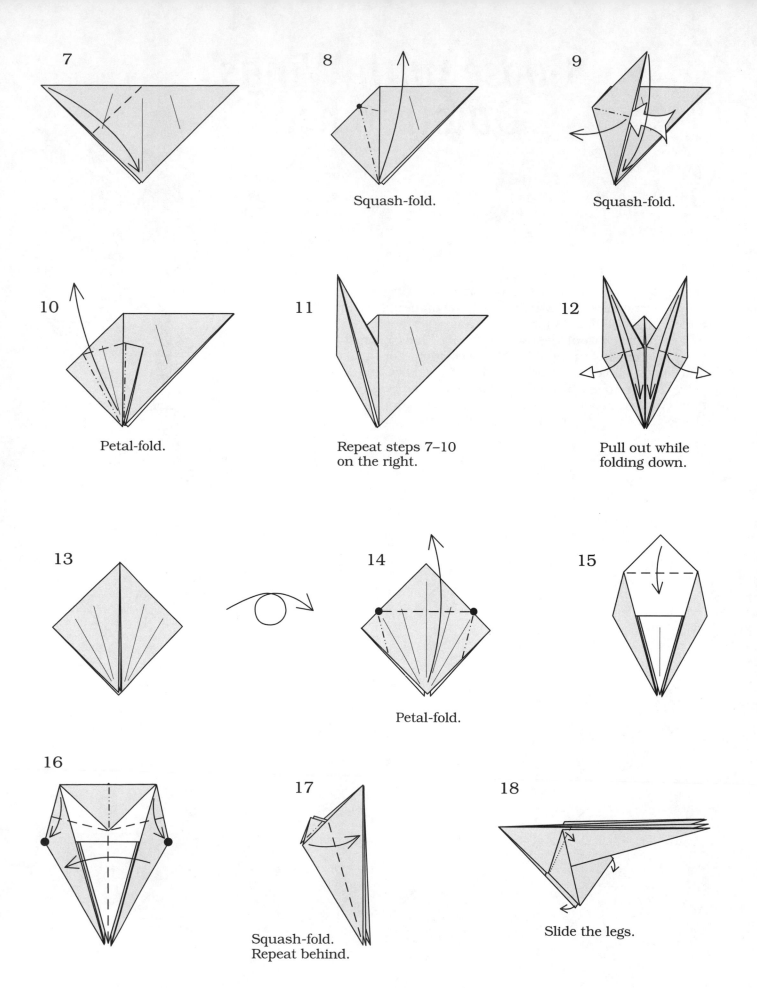

7

8

Squash-fold.

9

Squash-fold.

10

Petal-fold.

11

Repeat steps 7–10 on the right.

12

Pull out while folding down.

13

14

Petal-fold.

15

16

17

Squash-fold. Repeat behind.

18

Slide the legs.

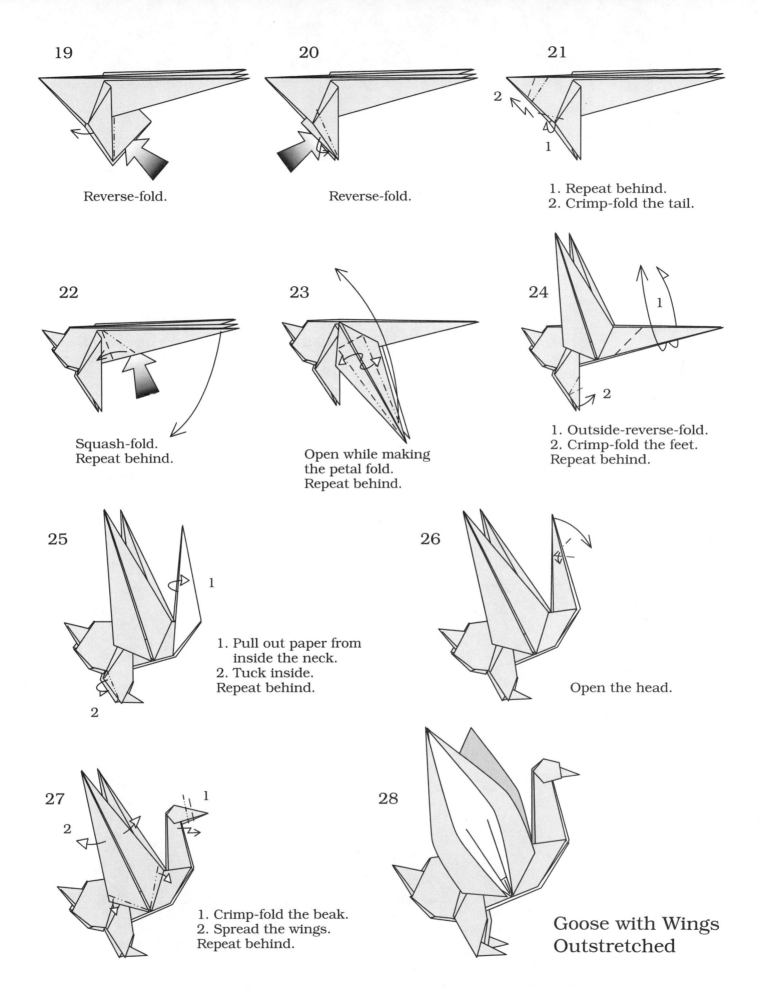

19

Reverse-fold.

20

Reverse-fold.

21

1. Repeat behind.
2. Crimp-fold the tail.

22

Squash-fold.
Repeat behind.

23

Open while making
the petal fold.
Repeat behind.

24

1. Outside-reverse-fold.
2. Crimp-fold the feet.
Repeat behind.

25

1. Pull out paper from
   inside the neck.
2. Tuck inside.
Repeat behind.

26

Open the head.

27

1. Crimp-fold the beak.
2. Spread the wings.
Repeat behind.

28

Goose with Wings
Outstretched

Pigeon

Pigeons are found all over the world. The most beautiful and colorful ones are found in Asia and Australasia. Pigeons spend much time around trees and eat seeds, fruits, and buds. These birds are powerful fliers with excellent homing abilities.

1

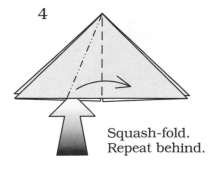

Fold and unfold.

2

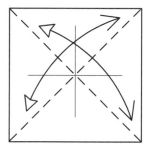

Fold and unfold.

3

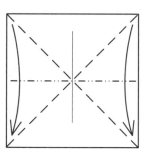

4

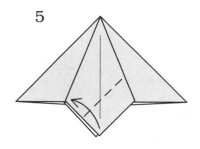

Squash-fold.
Repeat behind.

5

Pull out.

6

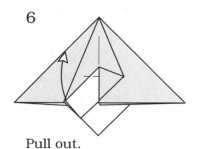

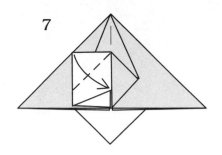

7

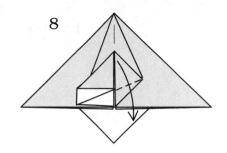

8

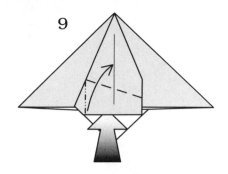

9

Squash-fold.

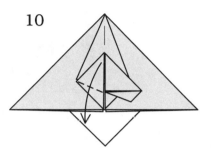

10

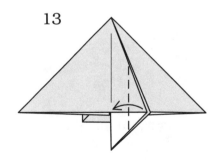

11

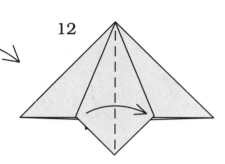

12

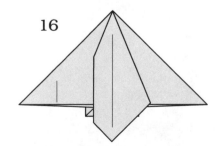

13

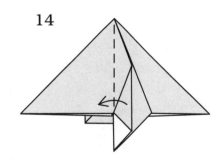

14

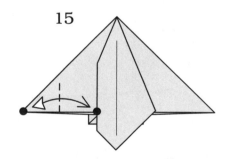

15

Fold and unfold.

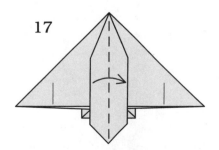

16

Repeat steps 12–15
on the right.

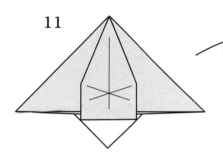

17

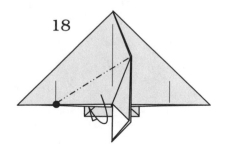

18

Pigeon 51

19

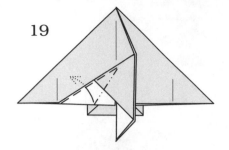

Squash-fold the white
layer from inside.

20

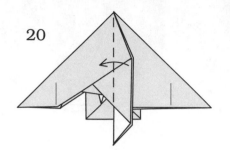
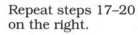

21

Repeat steps 17–20
on the right.

22

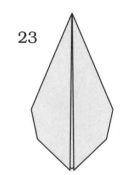

23

24

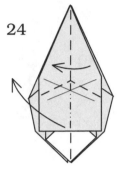

25

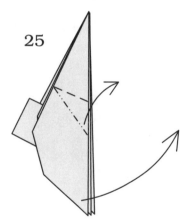

Squash-fold.
Repeat behind.

26

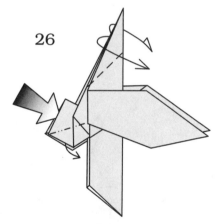

Reverse-fold at the legs.
Outside-reverse-fold the neck.

27

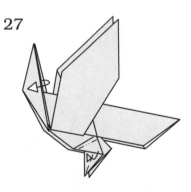

Pull out at the neck.
Repeat behind.

28

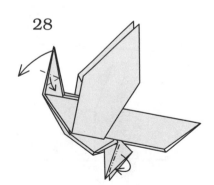

Open the head.
Reverse-fold the legs.

29

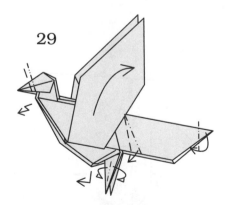

Cimp-fold the beak and tail. Thin
the legs and bend at the feet.
Curl the wings. Repeat behind.

30

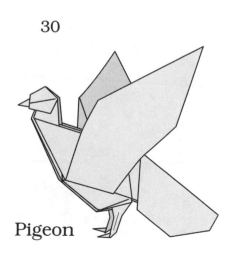

Pigeon

Hummingbird

Hummingbirds are small, brightly colored birds. The greatest number of species live in South America. About 12 species are found regularly in the United States and Canada. Most hummingbirds are small. The largest, the *Patagona gigas* of western South America, is only about 20 centimeters long. The smallest, the *Mellisuga helenae* of Cuba is slightly more than 5.5 cm. There are about 320 species of these brightly colored birds including the Coquette, Fairy, Hill Star, Wood Star, Sapphire, Topaz, Sun Gem, and Sylph.

7   Hummingbird

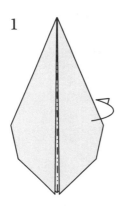

1

Begin with step 23 of the pigeon.

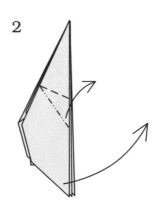

2

Squash-fold.
Repeat behind.

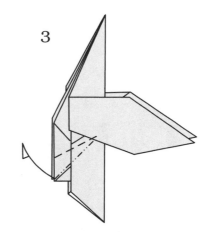

3

Crimp-fold.

4

Thin the leg and reverse-fold the tail. Repeat behind.

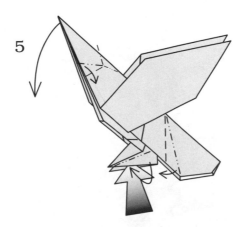

5

The fold for the head is similar to the crimp fold. Reverse-fold the legs and crimp-fold the tail.

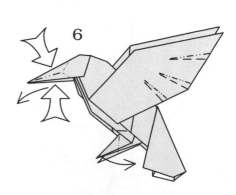

6

Thin and curl the beak, reverse-fold the feet, pleat along the wings, and spread the tail. Repeat behind.

Vulture

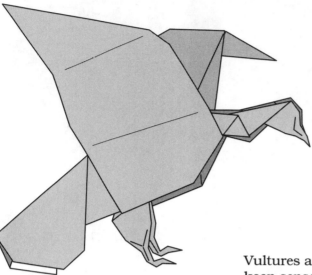

Vultures are large birds that have excellent eyesight and a keen sense of smell. They can be found in temperate and tropical regions and have broad eating habits, consuming carrion and garbage, but rarely live animals. On occasion, however, they catch helpless live prey like lambs and turtles. Vultures often roost and nest in groups on cliffs, in tall trees, or on the ground. They lay one or two eggs and incubate them for seven or eight weeks. Types of vultures include Black, King, Egyptian, Griffon, Turkey, and Palm-Nut.

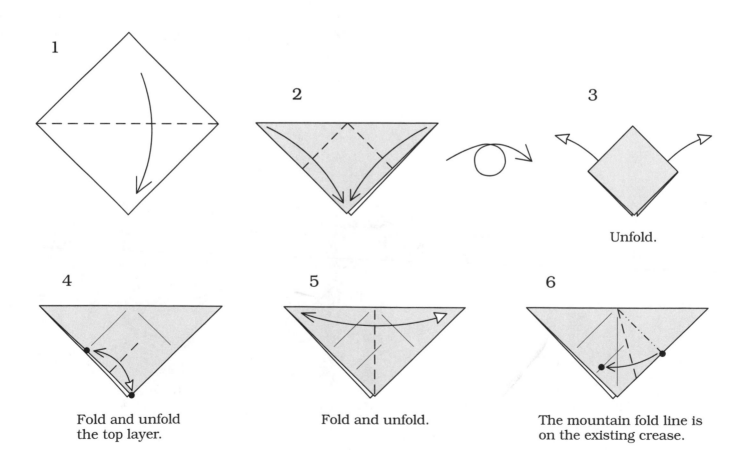

1

2

3

Unfold.

4

Fold and unfold the top layer.

5

Fold and unfold.

6

The mountain fold line is on the existing crease.

7

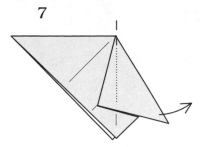

Slide so the left side
meets the center line.

8

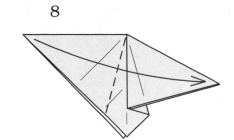

9

10

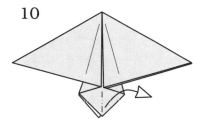

Pull out to unlock
the upper corner.

11

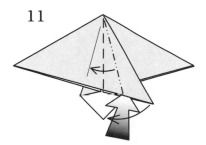

Squash-fold.

12

Petal-fold. The mountain
folds refer to hidden layers.

13

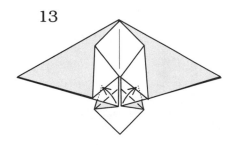

14

Fold and unfold.

15

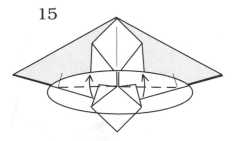

This is a view of
the inner layer.

16

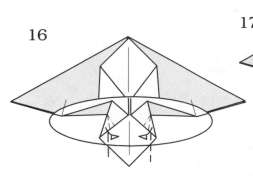

17

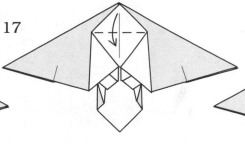

18

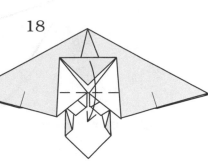

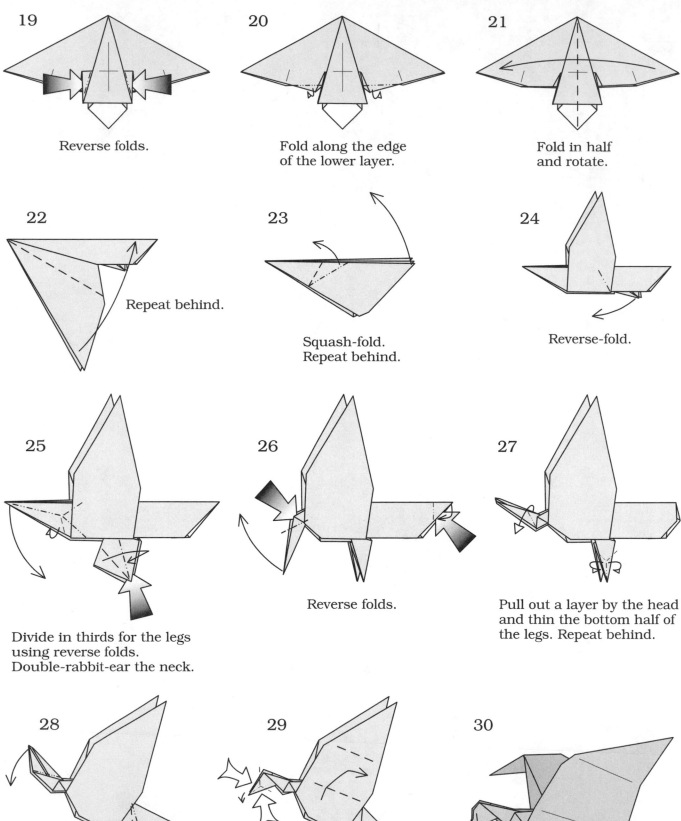

19

Reverse folds.

20

Fold along the edge of the lower layer.

21

Fold in half and rotate.

22

Repeat behind.

23

Squash-fold. Repeat behind.

24

Reverse-fold.

25

Divide in thirds for the legs using reverse folds. Double-rabbit-ear the neck.

26

Reverse folds.

27

Pull out a layer by the head and thin the bottom half of the legs. Repeat behind.

28

Reverse-fold the head, crimp-fold the tail, and bend the feet. Repeat behind.

29

Pinch and curl the beak, curl the foot, and spread the wings. Repeat behind.

30

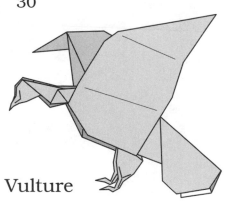

Vulture

Robin

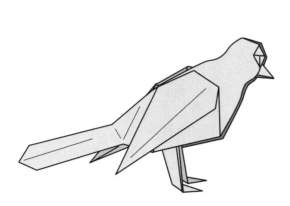

The robin lives in open woodlands, forest edges, gardens, and city parks. Robins can build nests from mud, grass, and twigs. The chicks stay in the nest for about two weeks. After the chicks leave the nest, the male parent feeds them and teaches them to pull worms from the ground. Their appearance is often seen as a sign of Spring.

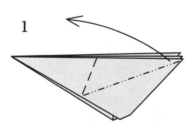

1

Begin with step 23 of the vulture. Squash-fold. Repeat behind.

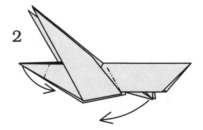

2

Reverse folds.

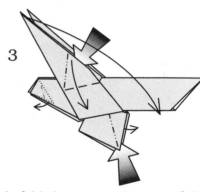

3

Squash-fold the wings. Reverse-fold the beak. Reverse-fold at an angle of about two-thirds for the legs. Repeat behind.

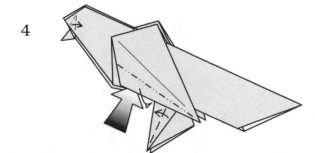

4

Squash-fold to form the eyes. Reverse-fold the wing. Repeat behind.

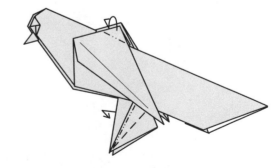

5

Thin the legs with reverse folds. Repeat behind.

6

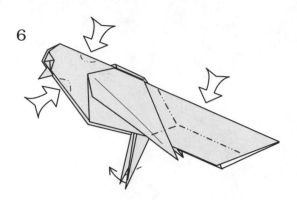

Reverse-fold the feet, form the tail with a three-dimensional double-rabbit-ear, and curve the neck. Repeat behind.

7

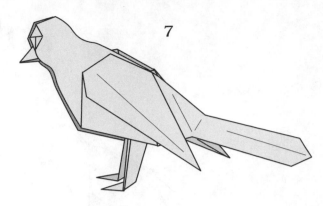

Robin

Robin with Wings Outstretched

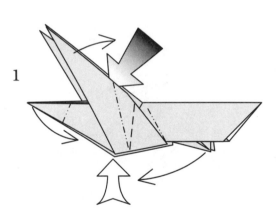

1

Begin with step 2 from above. Squash-fold the wings. Repeat behind.

2

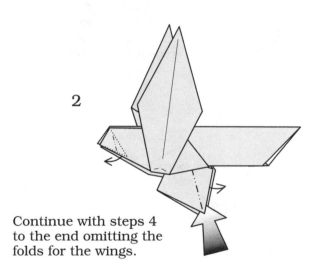

Continue with steps 4 to the end omitting the folds for the wings.

3

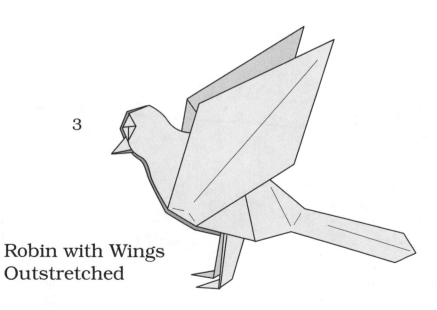

Robin with Wings Outstretched

Crane

Cranes are beautiful long-legged and long-necked birds. They often have decorative plumes on their heads. These social birds migrate in large flocks. Some species are rare and are bred in sanctuaries. Cranes have been incorporated into the myths and legends of many cultures, especially those in the Orient.

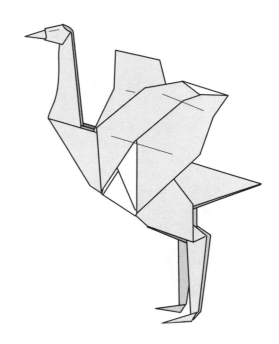

1

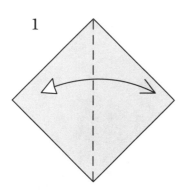

Fold and unfold.

2

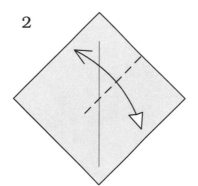

Fold and unfold.

3

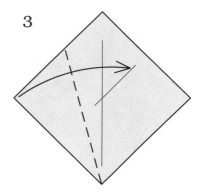

Fold the corner to the line.

4

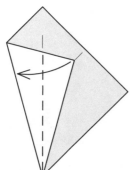

5

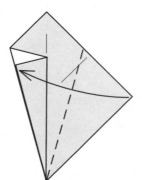

6

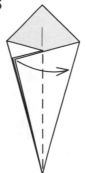

7

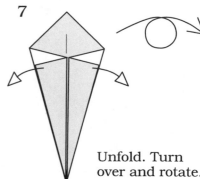

Unfold. Turn over and rotate.

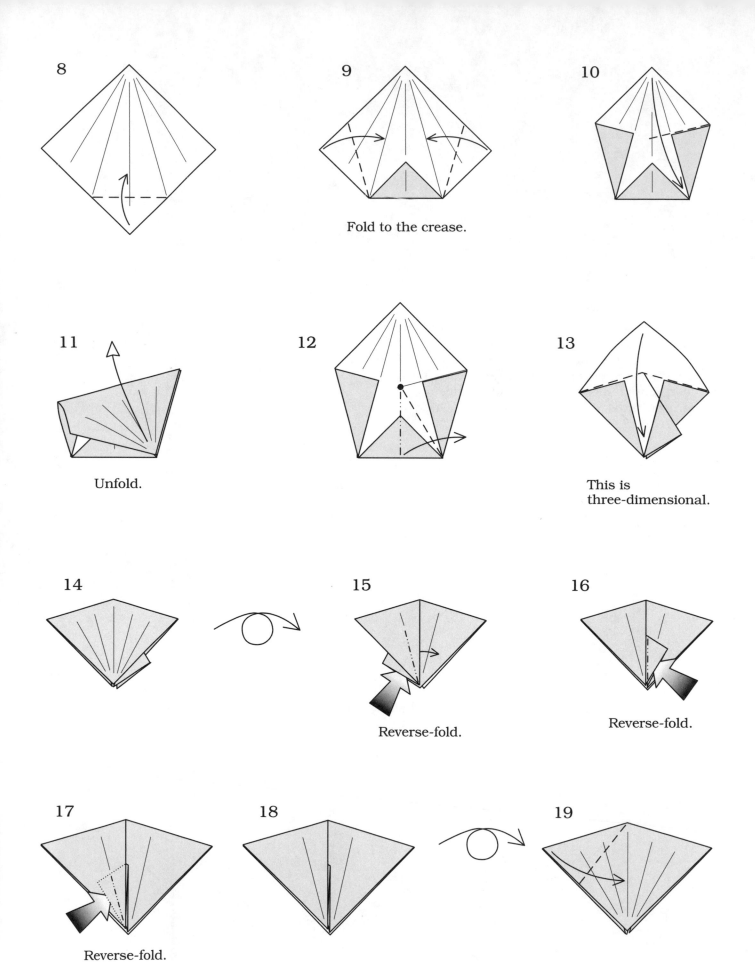

8

9

Fold to the crease.

10

11

Unfold.

12

13

This is
three-dimensional.

14

15

Reverse-fold.

16

Reverse-fold.

17

Reverse-fold.

18

19

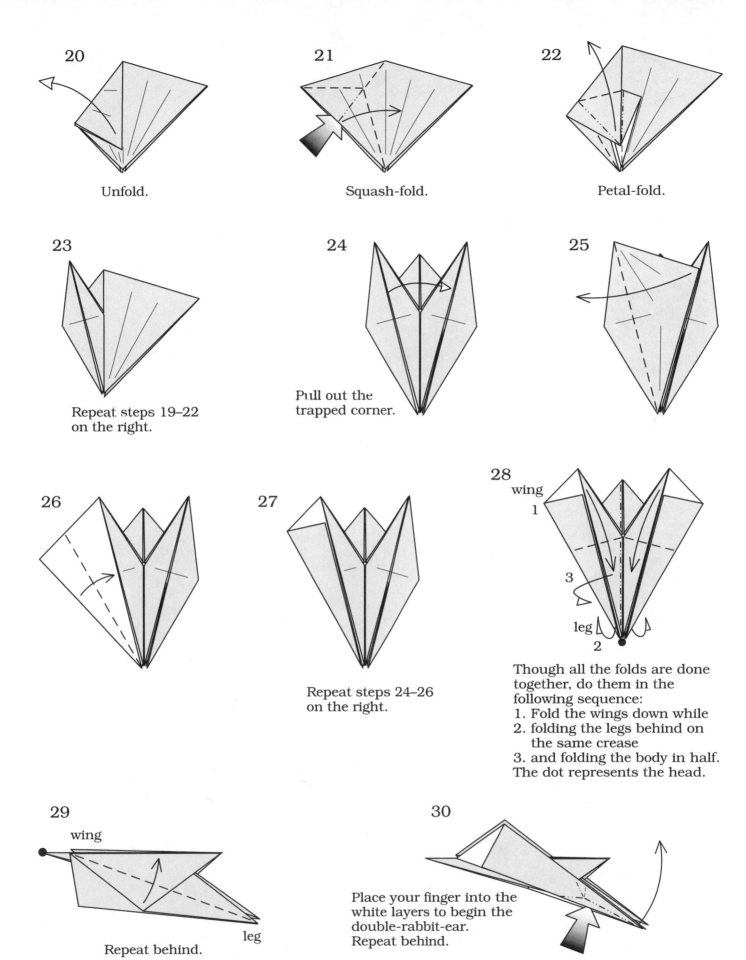

20

Unfold.

21

Squash-fold.

22

Petal-fold.

23

Repeat steps 19–22
on the right.

24

Pull out the
trapped corner.

25

26

27

Repeat steps 24–26
on the right.

28

wing

1

3

leg

2

Though all the folds are done
together, do them in the
following sequence:
1. Fold the wings down while
2. folding the legs behind on
   the same crease
3. and folding the body in half.
The dot represents the head.

29

wing

leg

Repeat behind.

30

Place your finger into the
white layers to begin the
double-rabbit-ear.
Repeat behind.

Crane 61

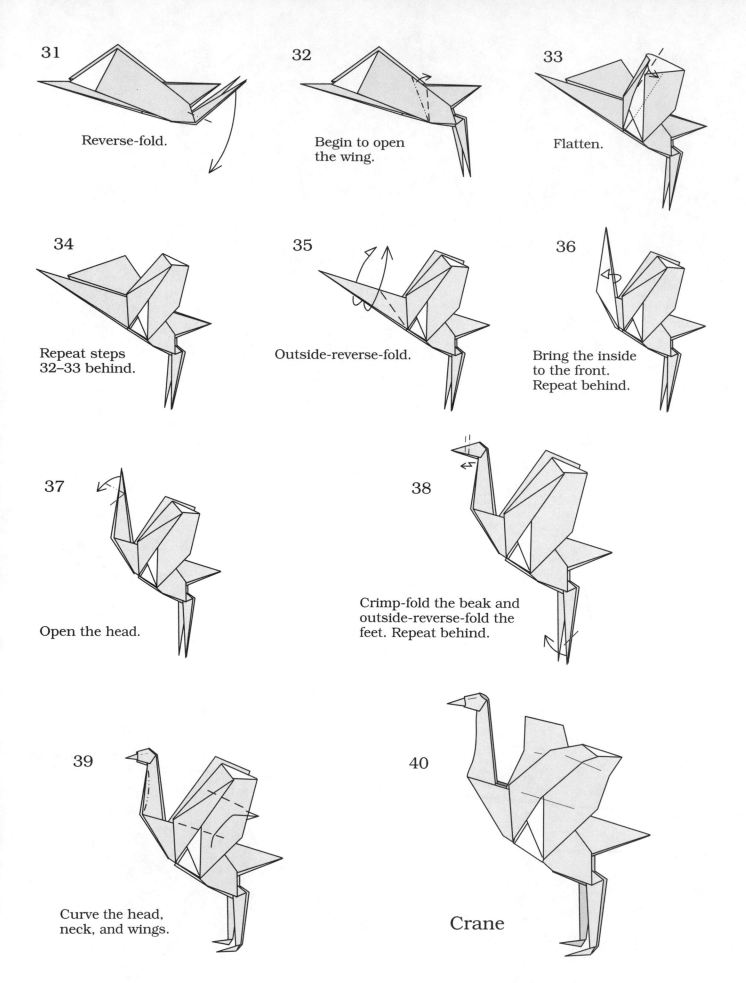

31 Reverse-fold.

32 Begin to open the wing.

33 Flatten.

34 Repeat steps 32–33 behind.

35 Outside-reverse-fold.

36 Bring the inside to the front. Repeat behind.

37 Open the head.

38 Crimp-fold the beak and outside-reverse-fold the feet. Repeat behind.

39 Curve the head, neck, and wings.

40 Crane

Parrot

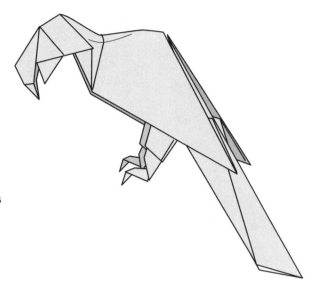

The term "parrot" is a general one that applies to about 300 different species. Parrots are for the most part mild mannered; however some species have been known to attack sheep and damage crops. In general, these elegant creatures live in warm, tropical climates and feed on fruits and seeds, among other treats.

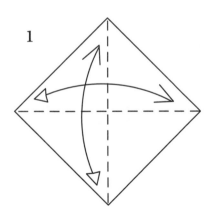

1

Fold and unfold.

2

Crease lightly.

3

4

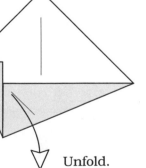

Unfold.

5

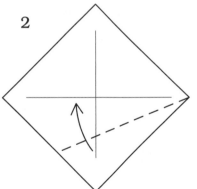

6

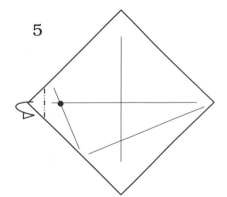

Fold and unfold.

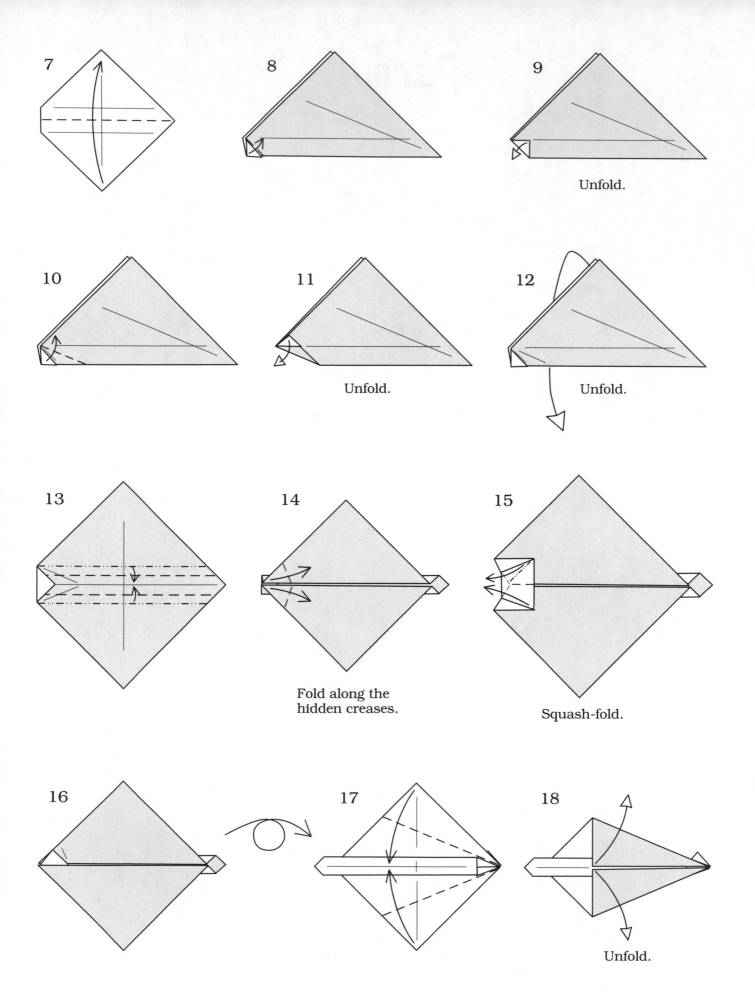

7

8

9

Unfold.

10

11

Unfold.

12

Unfold.

13

14

Fold along the
hidden creases.

15

Squash-fold.

16

17

18

Unfold.

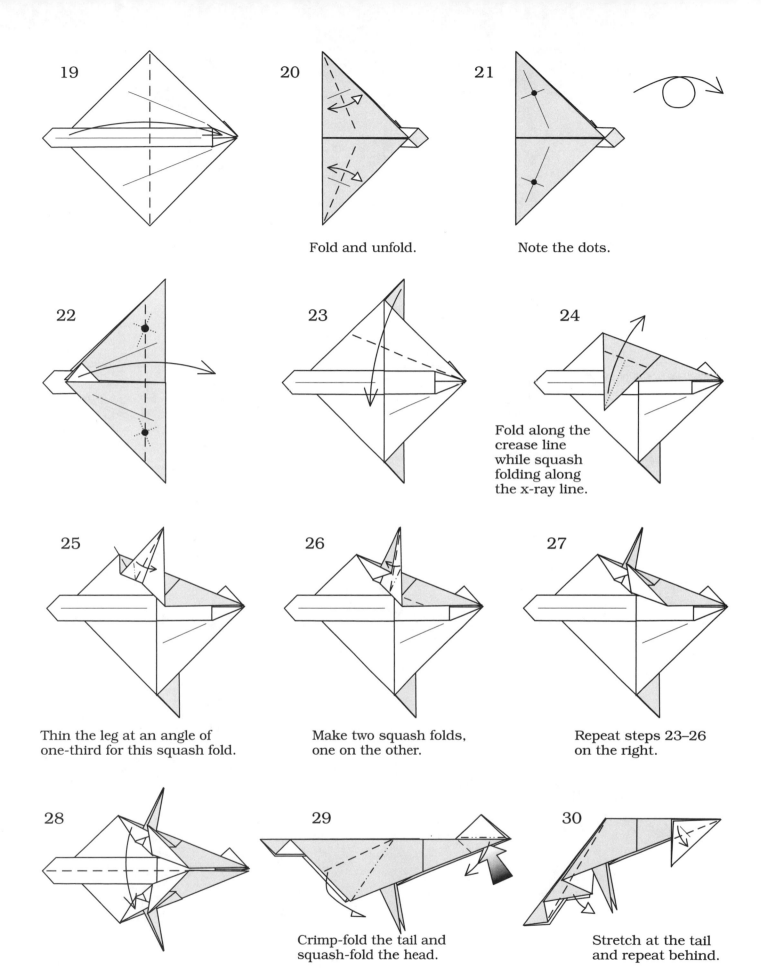

19

20

Fold and unfold.

21

Note the dots.

22

23

24

Fold along the
crease line
while squash
folding along
the x-ray line.

25

Thin the leg at an angle of
one-third for this squash fold.

26

Make two squash folds,
one on the other.

27

Repeat steps 23–26
on the right.

28

29

Crimp-fold the tail and
squash-fold the head.

30

Stretch at the tail
and repeat behind.

Parrot 65

31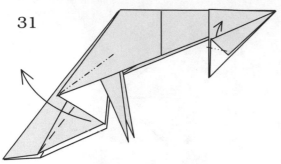

Reverse-fold the beak and at the tail. Repeat behind at the tail.

32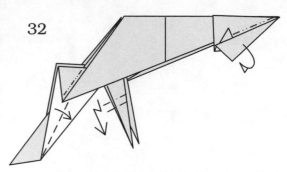

Reverse-fold at the tail, crimp-fold the legs, and fold inside at the head. Repeat behind.

33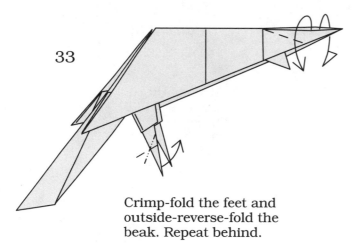

Crimp-fold the feet and outside-reverse-fold the beak. Repeat behind.

34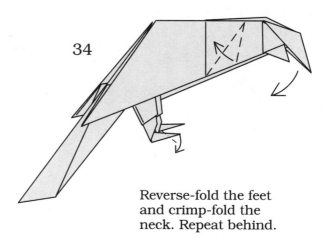

Reverse-fold the feet and crimp-fold the neck. Repeat behind.

35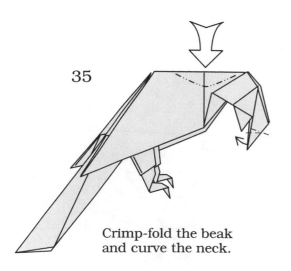

Crimp-fold the beak and curve the neck.

36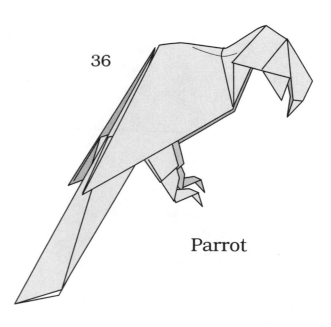

Parrot

Stork

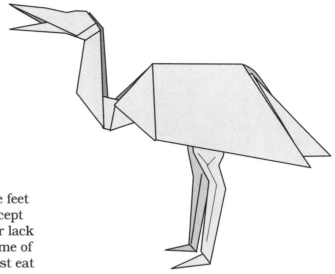

Storks are fairly large birds, between two to five feet in height, which live on all of the continents except Antarctica. Storks are voiceless or nearly so, for lack of a fully developed syrinx (vocal organ), but some of them clatter their bills loudly when excited. Most eat small fish caught in shallow water.

1

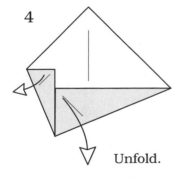

Fold and unfold.

2

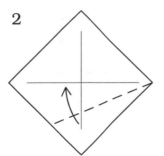

Crease lightly.

3

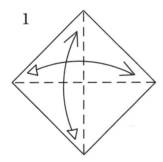

4

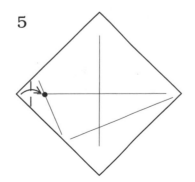

Unfold.

5

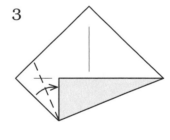

6

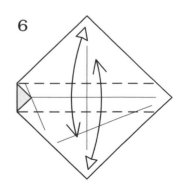

Fold and unfold.

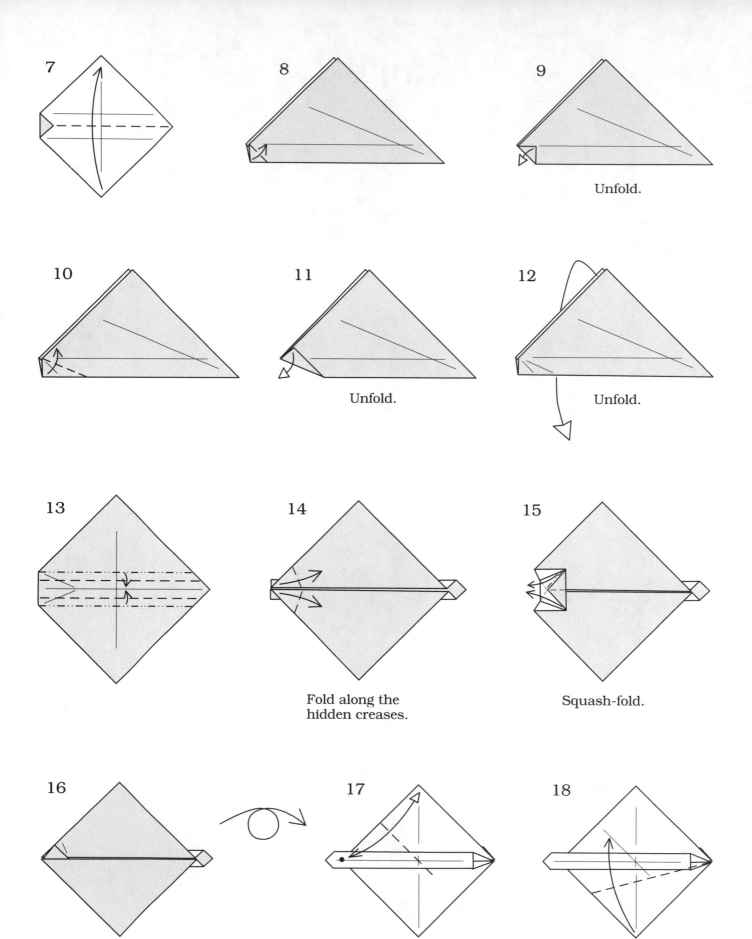

7

8

9

Unfold.

10

11

Unfold.

12

Unfold.

13

14

Fold along the
hidden creases.

15

Squash-fold.

16

17

Fold and unfold.

18

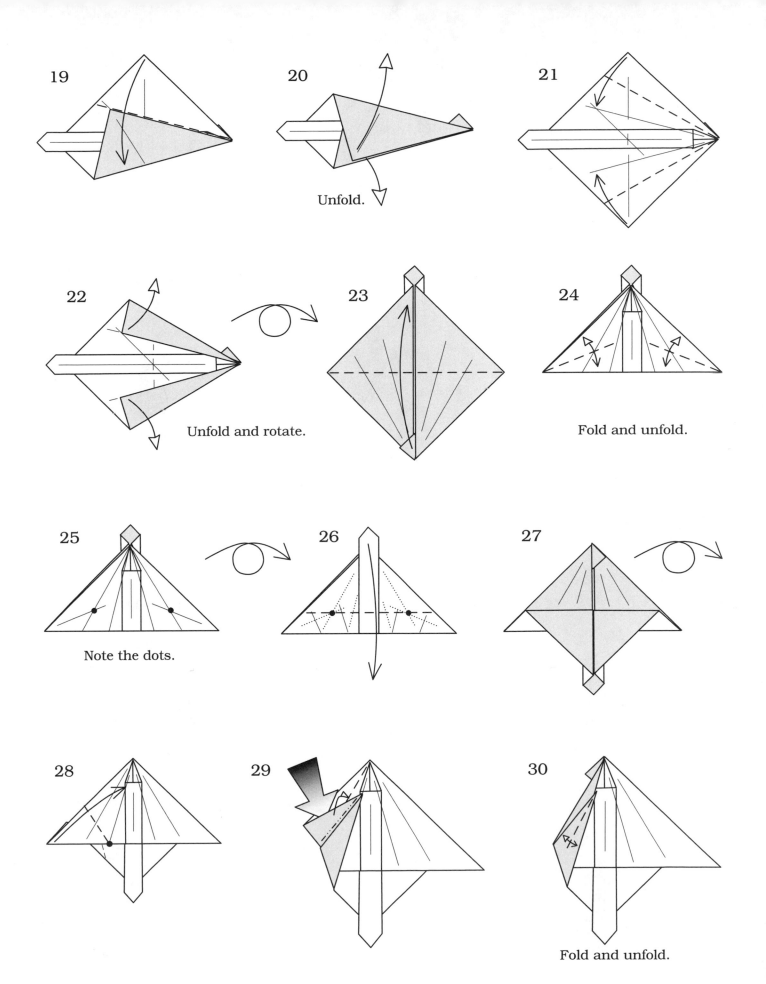

19

20

Unfold.

21

22

Unfold and rotate.

23

24

Fold and unfold.

25

Note the dots.

26

27

28

29

30

Fold and unfold.

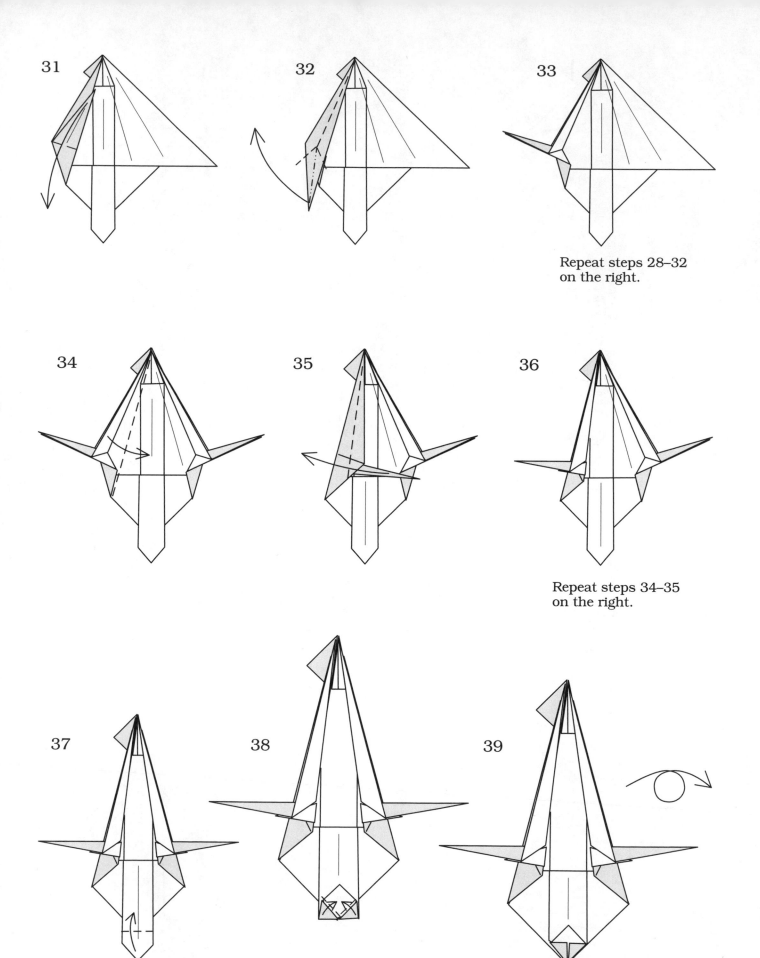

31

32

33

Repeat steps 28–32
on the right.

34

35

36

Repeat steps 34–35
on the right.

37

38

39

40

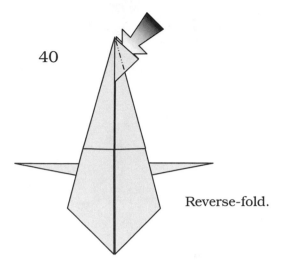

Reverse-fold.

41

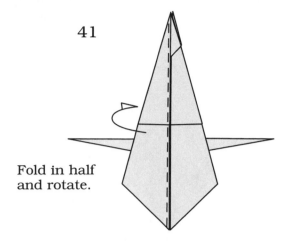

Fold in half
and rotate.

42

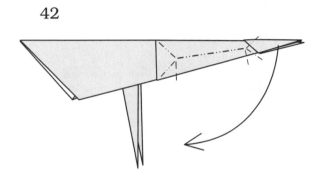

Double-rabbit-ear on
the left and right.

43

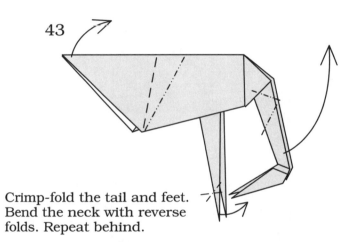

Crimp-fold the tail and feet.
Bend the neck with reverse
folds. Repeat behind.

44

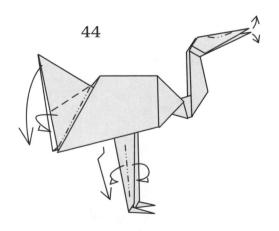

Crimp-fold the tail,
thin and bend the
legs, open the beak.

45

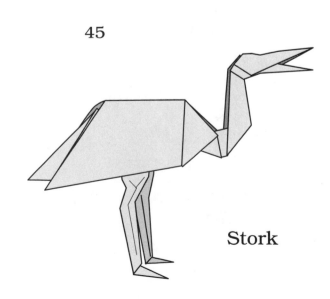

Stork

Scavenger Beetle

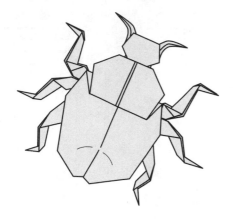

The scavenger beetle is a large beetle that can be found feeding on dead plants at the edge of ponds. The scavenger beetle has a distinctive ridge on its back. In order to breathe, it keeps an air bubble trapped underneath its body while it is in the water.

1

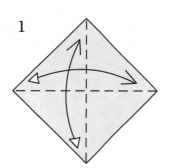

Fold and unfold.

2

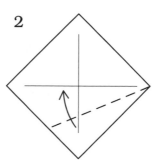

Crease lightly.

3

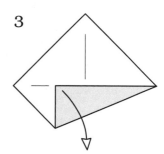

Unfold.

4

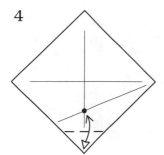

Fold and unfold.

5

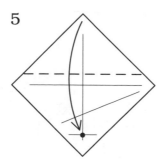

6

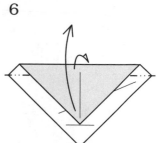

7

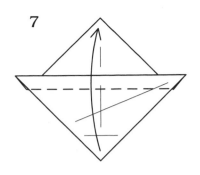

8

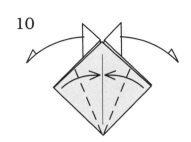

9

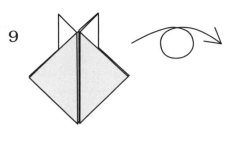

10

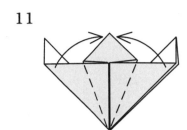

11

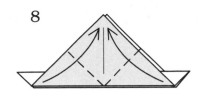

12

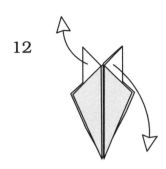

Unfold everything.

13

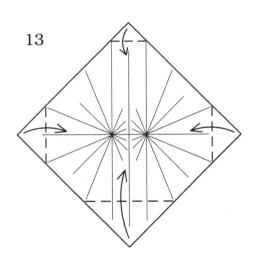

14

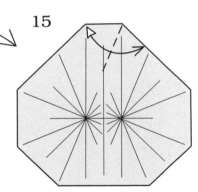

15

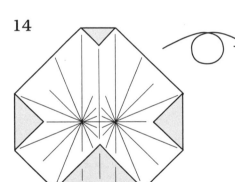

Fold and unfold.

16

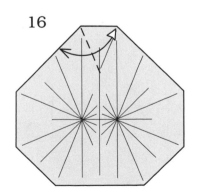

Fold and unfold.

17

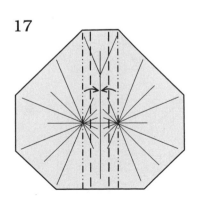

18

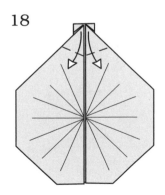

Fold along the hidden creases made in steps 15 and 16.

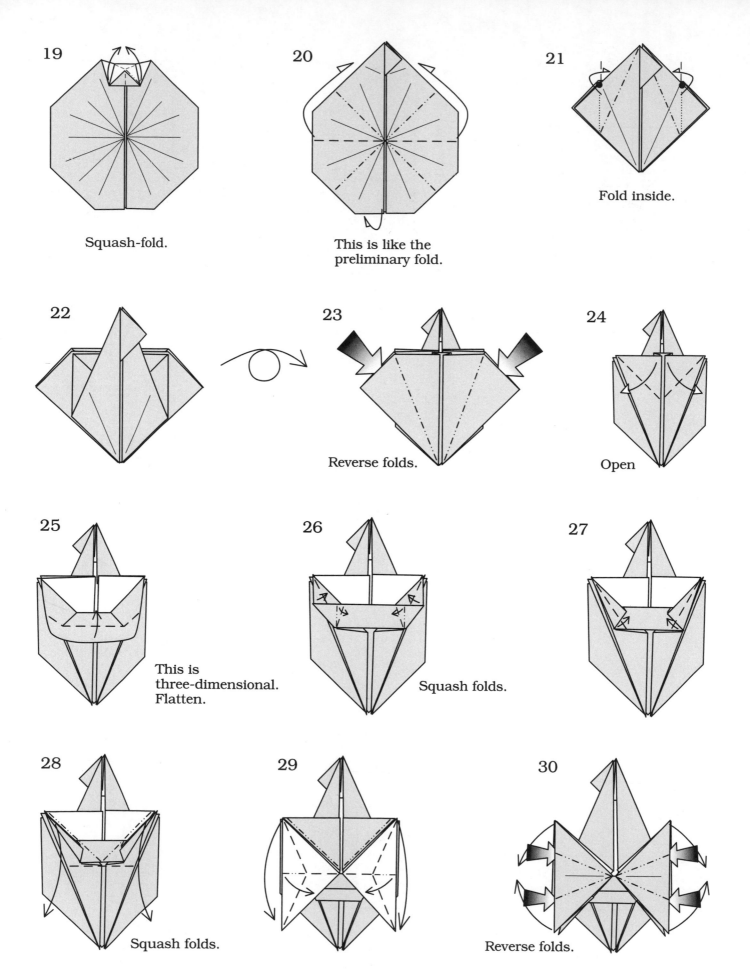

19

Squash-fold.

20

This is like the
preliminary fold.

21

Fold inside.

22

23

Reverse folds.

24

Open

25

This is
three-dimensional.
Flatten.

26

Squash folds.

27

28

Squash folds.

29

30

Reverse folds.

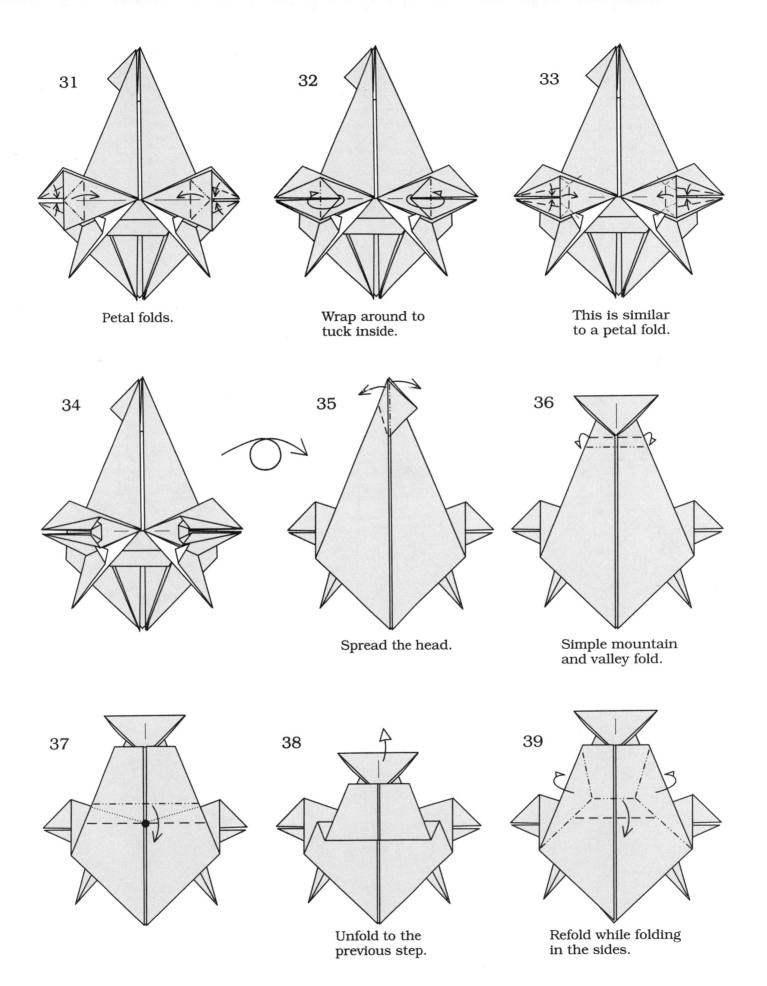

31

Petal folds.

32

Wrap around to
tuck inside.

33

This is similar
to a petal fold.

34

35

Spread the head.

36

Simple mountain
and valley fold.

37

38

Unfold to the
previous step.

39

Refold while folding
in the sides.

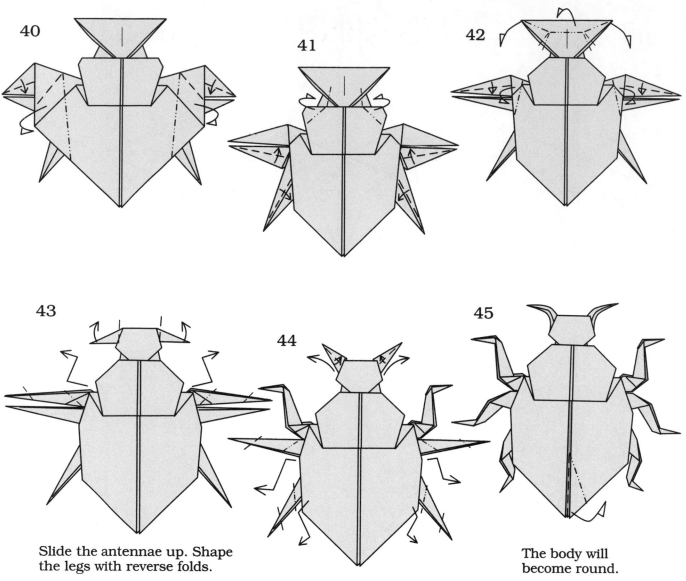

40

41

42

43

Slide the antennae up. Shape
the legs with reverse folds.

44

Thin and curl the antennae.
Continue bending the legs
with reverse folds.

45

The body will
become round.

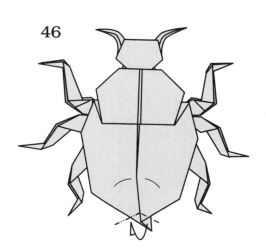

46

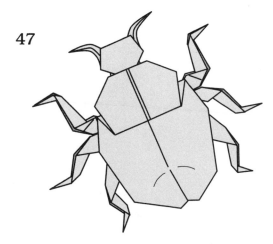

47

Scavenger Beetle

Ladybug

Ladybugs are small, brightly colored beetles. Generally under 1/4 inch long, they are oval in shape, have short legs, and are red or yellow with black spots or black with red or yellow spots. Ladybugs feed on destructive, plant-eating insects; adults are frequently used in pest control.

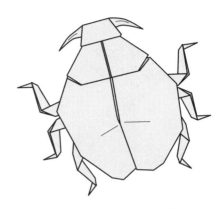

1

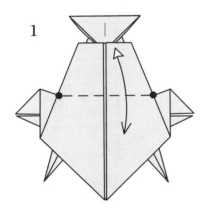

Begin with step 37 of the scavenger beetle. Fold and unfold.

2

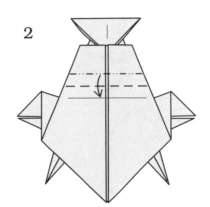

Fold to the crease.

3

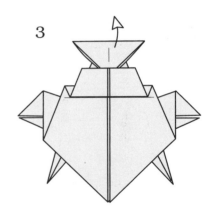

Unfold to the previous step.

4

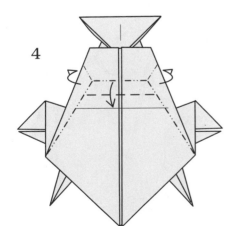

Refold while folding in the sides.

5

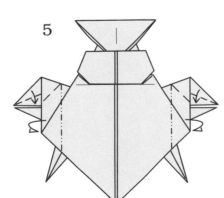

6

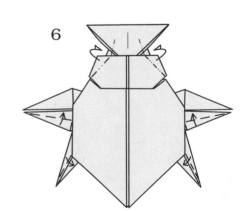

7

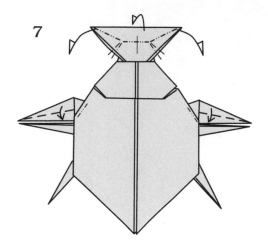

8

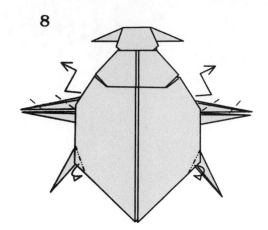

Shape the legs
with reverse folds.

9

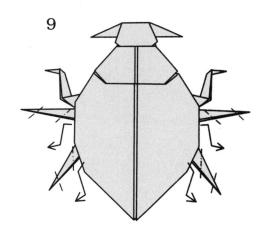

10

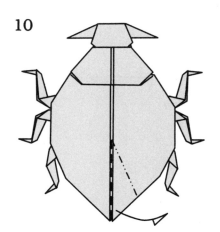

The body will
become round.

11

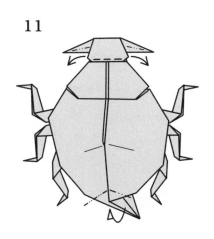

12

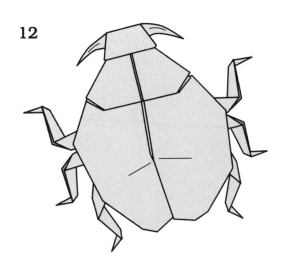

Ladybug

Fly

The fly is one of approximately 85,000 different insects known as dipterans. These creatures can be found just about anywhere on earth, from sub-Arctic conditions to the serene environment of the high mountains. The fly has an unremitting pursuit for food and drink; however, flies are one of the most important parts of the food chain.

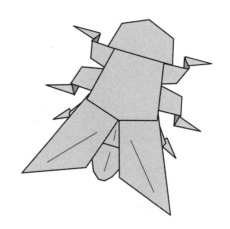

1

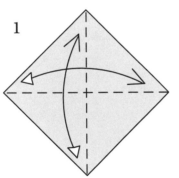

Fold and unfold.

2

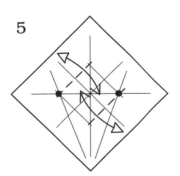

Kite-fold and unfold.

3

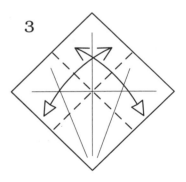

Fold and unfold.

4

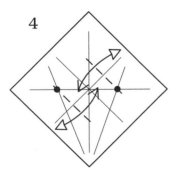

Fold and unfold.

5

Fold and unfold.

6

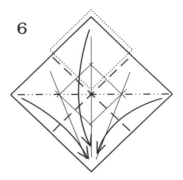

Note the upper square region has no crease marks from the kite-fold. Make a preliminary fold.

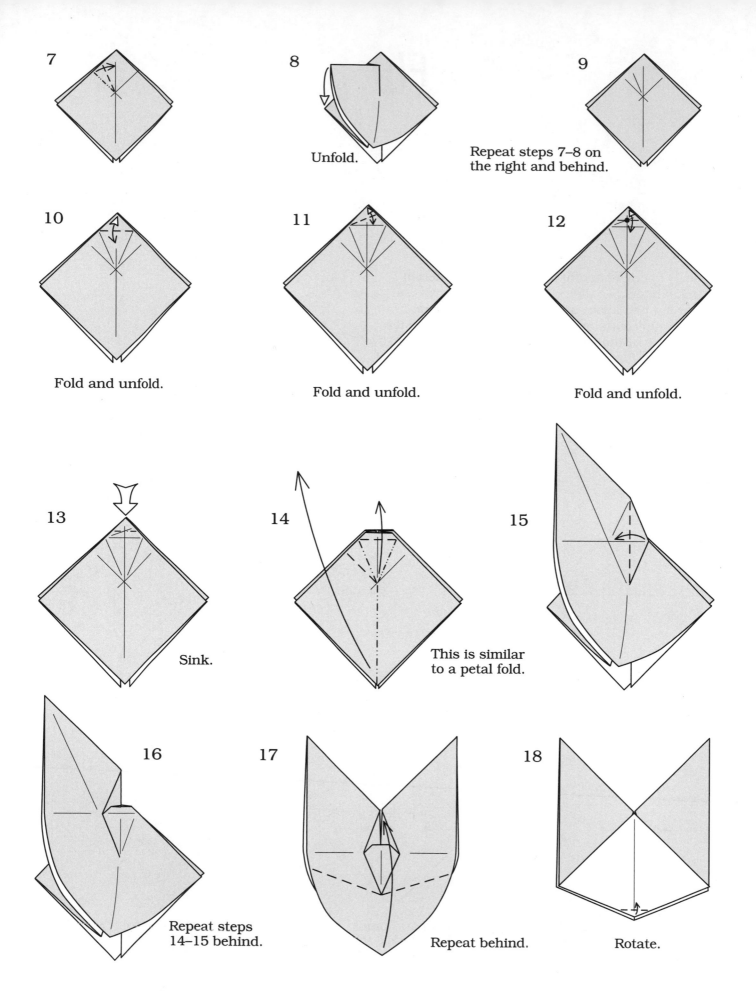

7

8

Unfold.

9

Repeat steps 7–8 on
the right and behind.

10

Fold and unfold.

11

Fold and unfold.

12

Fold and unfold.

13

Sink.

14

This is similar
to a petal fold.

15

16

Repeat steps
14–15 behind.

17

Repeat behind.

18

Rotate.

19

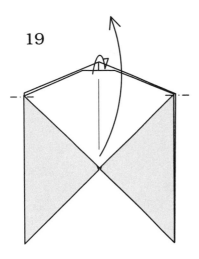

20

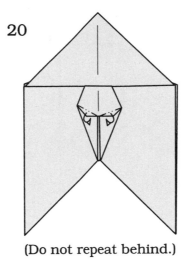

(Do not repeat behind.)

21

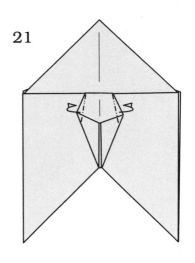

22

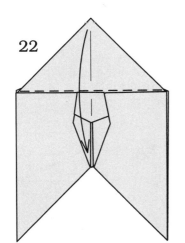

23

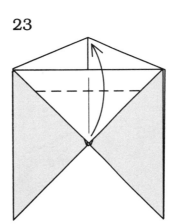

24

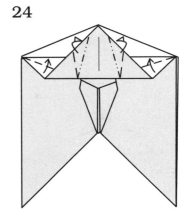

25

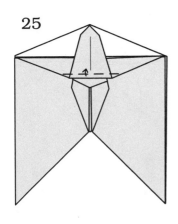

26

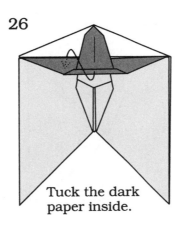

Tuck the dark paper inside.

27

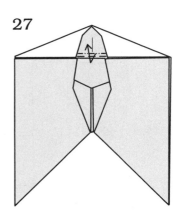

Fly 81

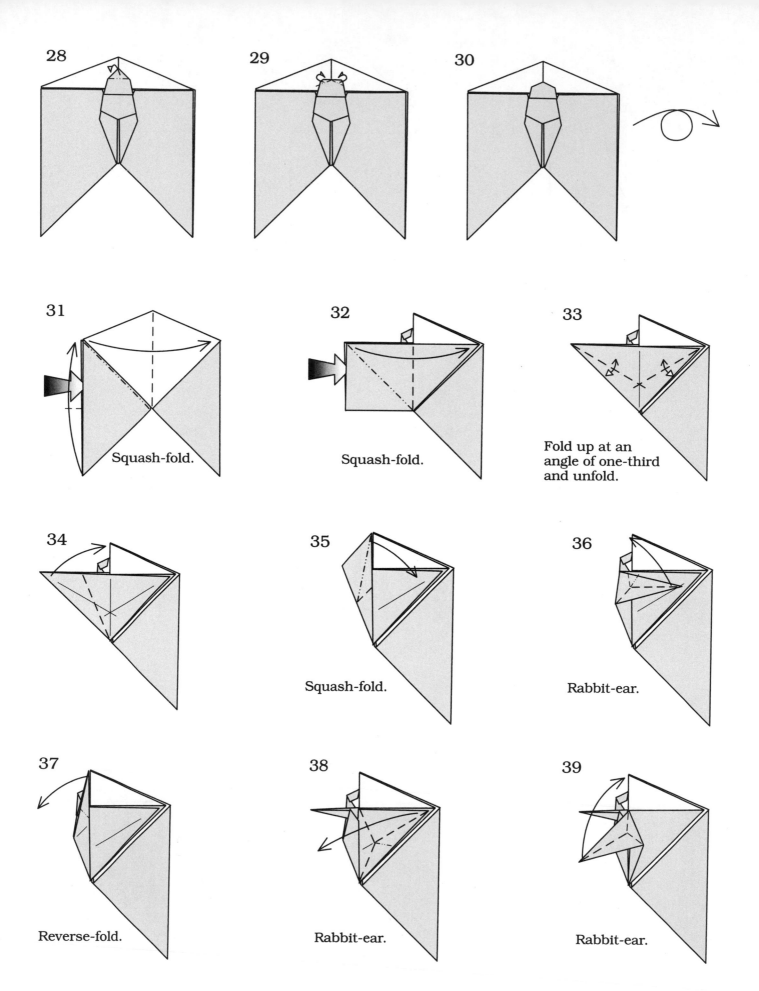

28

29

30

31

Squash-fold.

32

Squash-fold.

33

Fold up at an angle of one-third and unfold.

34

35

Squash-fold.

36

Rabbit-ear.

37

Reverse-fold.

38

Rabbit-ear.

39

Rabbit-ear.

40

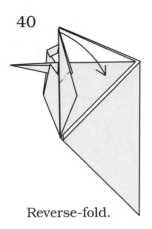

Reverse-fold.

41

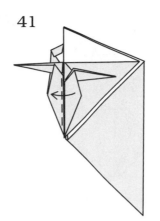

42

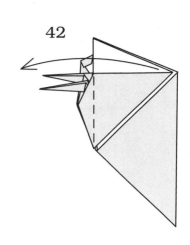

43

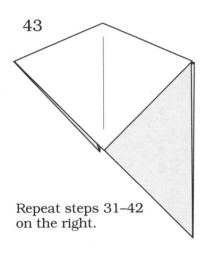

Repeat steps 31–42
on the right.

44

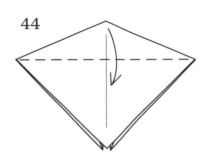

45

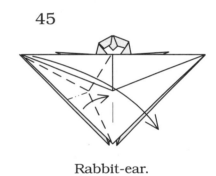

Rabbit-ear.

46

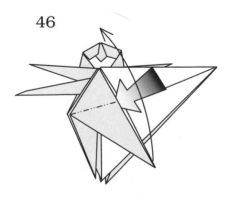

Squash-fold.

47

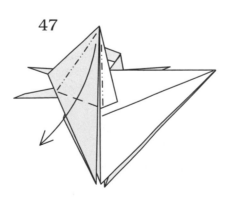

Petal-fold.

48

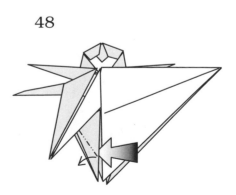

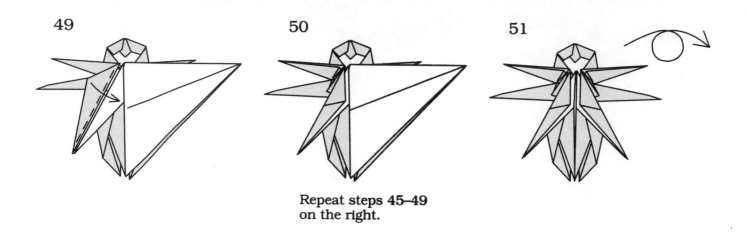

49 **50** **51**

Repeat steps **45–49**
on the right.

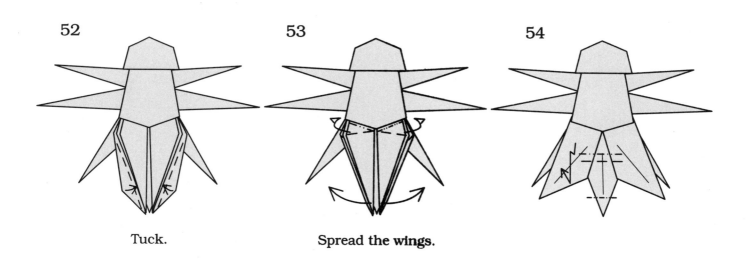

52 **53** **54**

Tuck. Spread the **wings**.

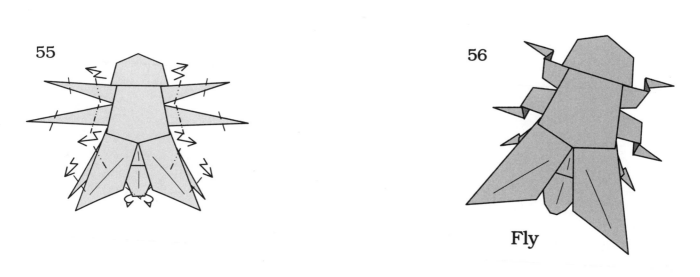

55 **56**

Fly

Spider

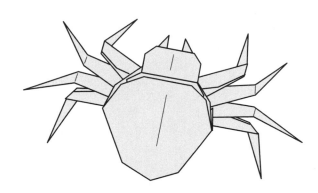

Spiders (arachnids) can be found all over the world. There are thousands of different kinds of spiders ranging in size and color. A female spider lays more than a thousand eggs at a time. When the eggs hatch, the baby spiders look like tiny versions of their full grown parents.

1

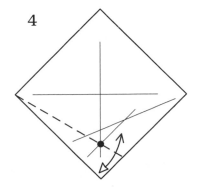

Fold and unfold.

2

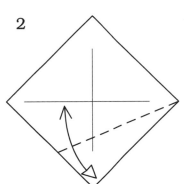

Fold and unfold.

3

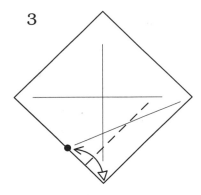

Folds the corner to the dot and unfold.

4

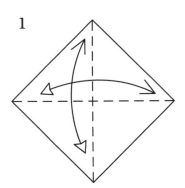

Folds through the dot and unfold.

5

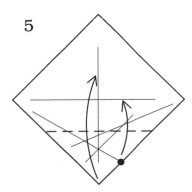

Fold up so the dot meets with the diagonal.

6

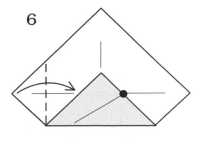

7

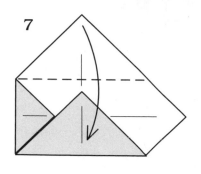

8

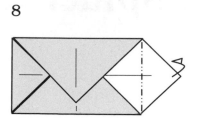

9

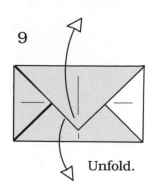

Unfold.

10

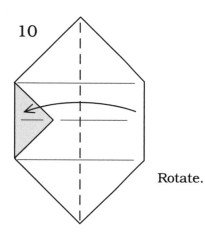

Rotate.

11

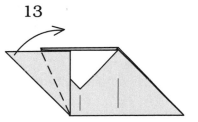

12

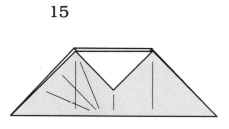

13

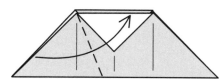

14

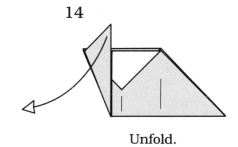

Unfold.

15

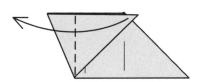

Repeat steps 11–14 on the right.

16

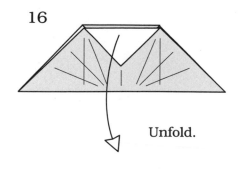

Unfold.

17

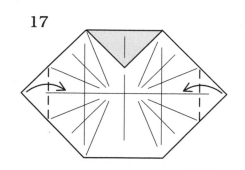

18

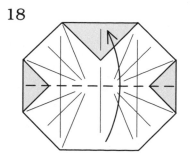

19

Crimp-fold.

20

Reverse-fold.

21

Repeat steps 19–20
on the right.

22

Reverse-fold.

23

Reverse-fold.

24

Unfold.

25

Reverse-fold.

26

Reverse-fold.

27

Reverse-fold.

28

Repeat steps 22–27 on
the remaining 5 places.

29

Squash-fold.

30

Squash-fold.

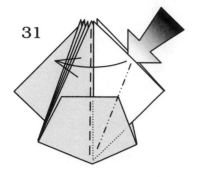

31

Squash-fold.
Repeat behind.

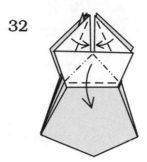

32

Petal-fold.
Repeat behind.

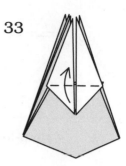

33

Repeat behind.

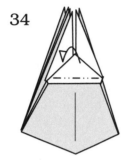

34

Repeat behind.

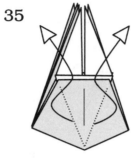

35

Unwrap the white paper.
Do not repeat behind.

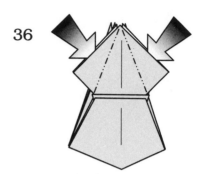

36

Reverse folds.

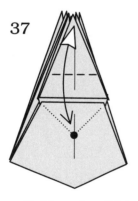

37

Fold and unfold.

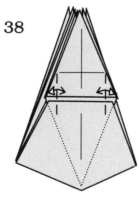

38

Fold and unfold.

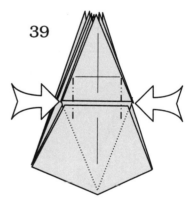

39

Sink.

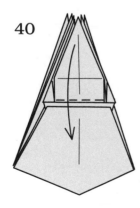

40

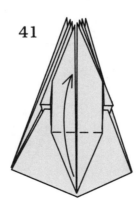

41

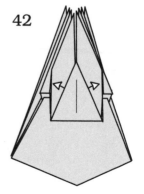

42

Pull out.

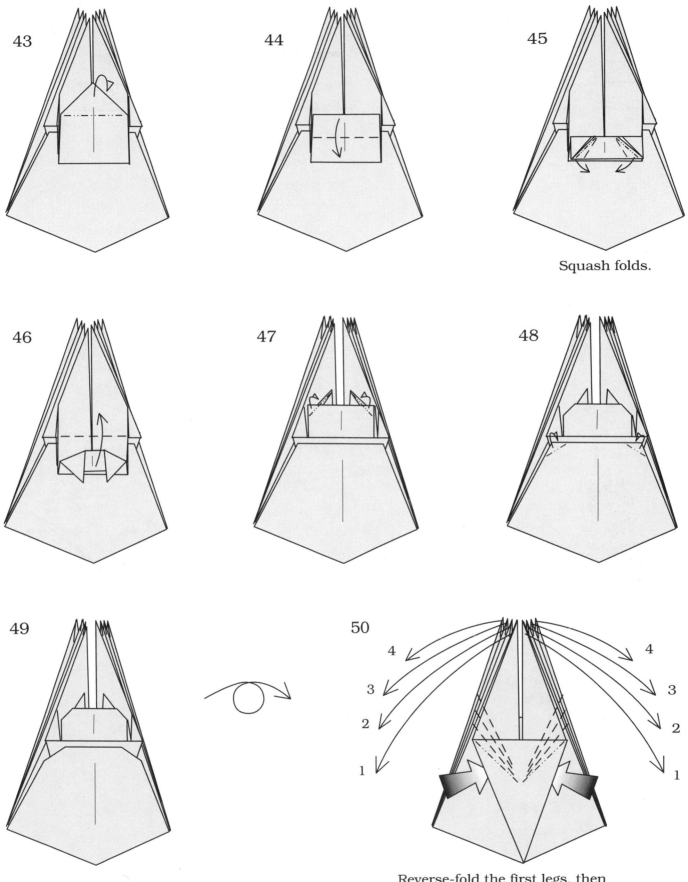

43

44

45

Squash folds.

46

47

48

49

50

4   4
3   3
2   2
1   1

Reverse-fold the first legs, then
valley-fold each other one with small
squash folds at the base of the legs.

Spider 89

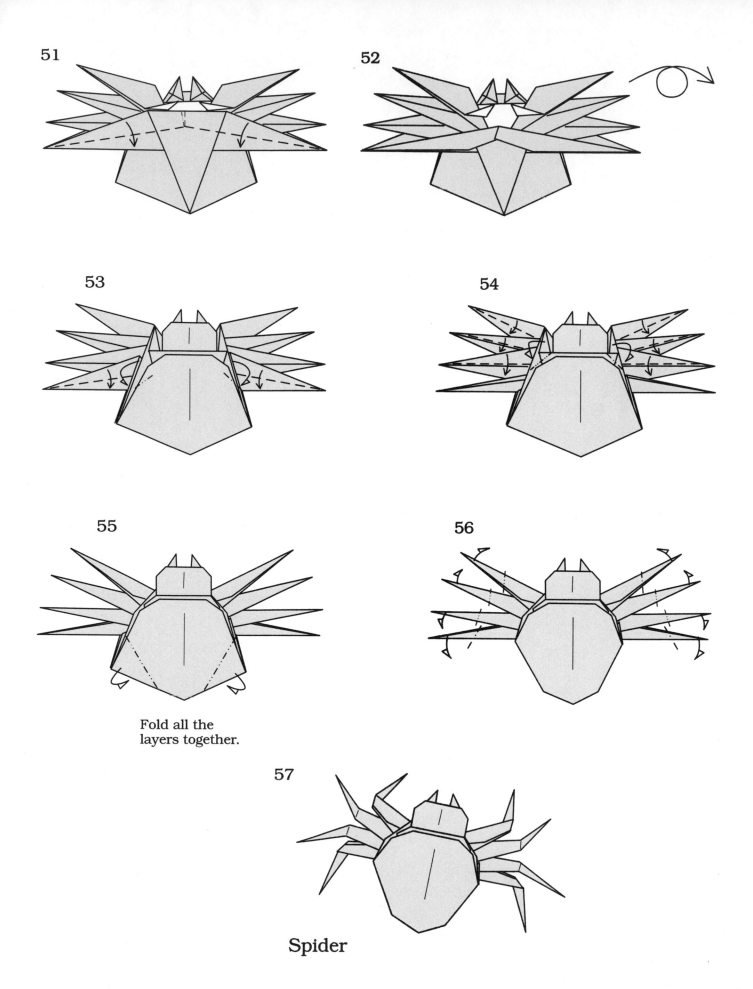

51

52

53

54

55

Fold all the
layers together.

56

57

Spider

Wasp

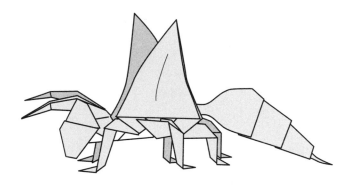

There are over 20,000 species of wasps. These stinging insects are thin between the thorax and abdomen. The adults feed on nectar while the larvae feed on insects. The most familiar wasps arc yellow jackets and hornets.

1

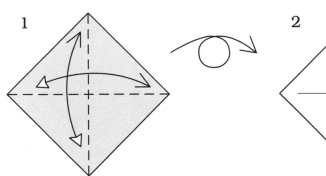

Fold and unfold.

2

Fold and unfold.

3

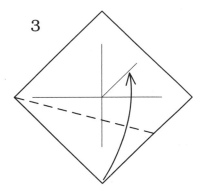

Folds the corner to the crease.

4

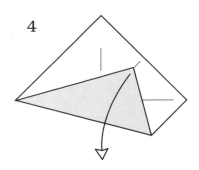

5

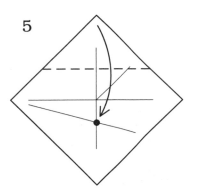

6

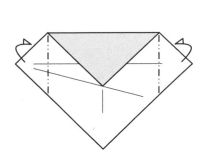

7

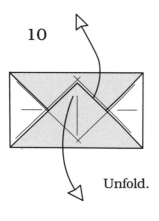

8

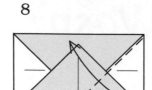

Fold and unfold.

9

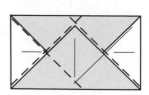

Fold and unfold
three more times.

10

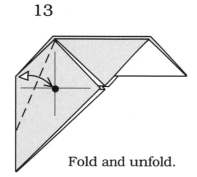

Unfold.

11

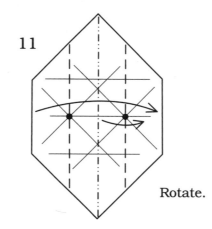

Rotate.

12

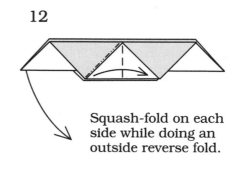

Squash-fold on each
side while doing an
outside reverse fold.

13

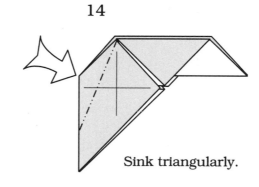

Fold and unfold.

14

Sink triangularly.

15

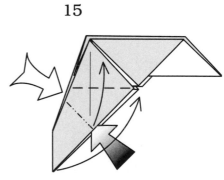

Squash-fold on each
side while doing a
stretched squash fold.

16

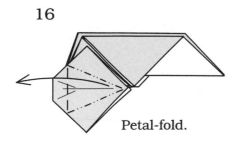

Petal-fold.

17

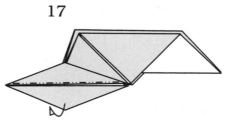

18

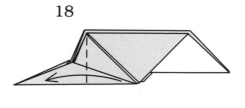

Repeat behind.

19

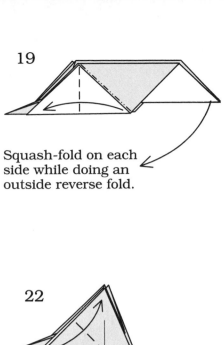

Squash-fold on each side while doing an outside reverse fold.

20

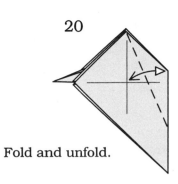

Fold and unfold.

21

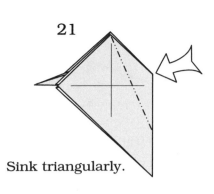

Sink triangularly.

22

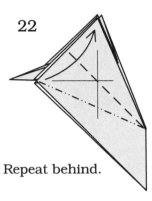

Repeat behind.

23

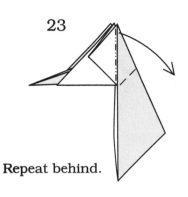

Repeat behind.

24

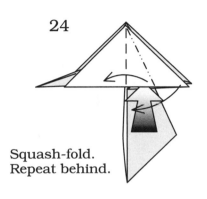

Squash-fold. Repeat behind.

25

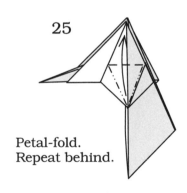

Petal-fold. Repeat behind.

26

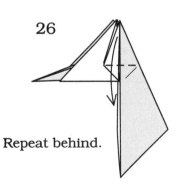

Repeat behind.

27

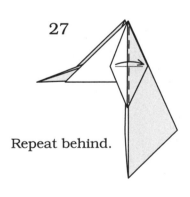

Repeat behind.

28

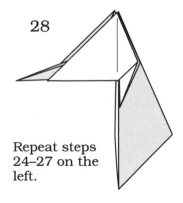

Repeat steps 24–27 on the left.

29

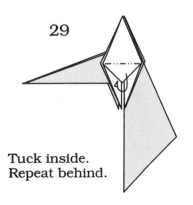

Tuck inside. Repeat behind.

30

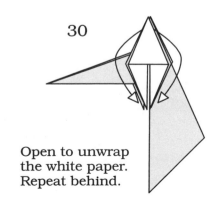

Open to unwrap the white paper. Repeat behind.

Wasp 93

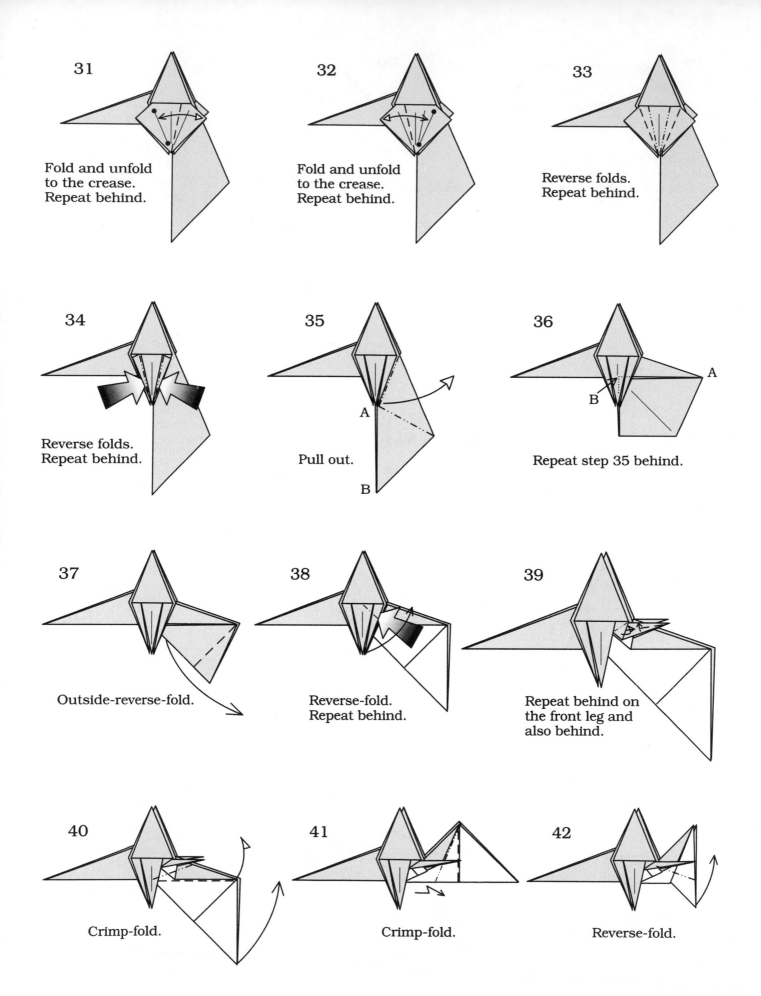

31 Fold and unfold to the crease. Repeat behind.

32 Fold and unfold to the crease. Repeat behind.

33 Reverse folds. Repeat behind.

34 Reverse folds. Repeat behind.

35 Pull out.

36 Repeat step 35 behind.

37 Outside-reverse-fold.

38 Reverse-fold. Repeat behind.

39 Repeat behind on the front leg and also behind.

40 Crimp-fold.

41 Crimp-fold.

42 Reverse-fold.

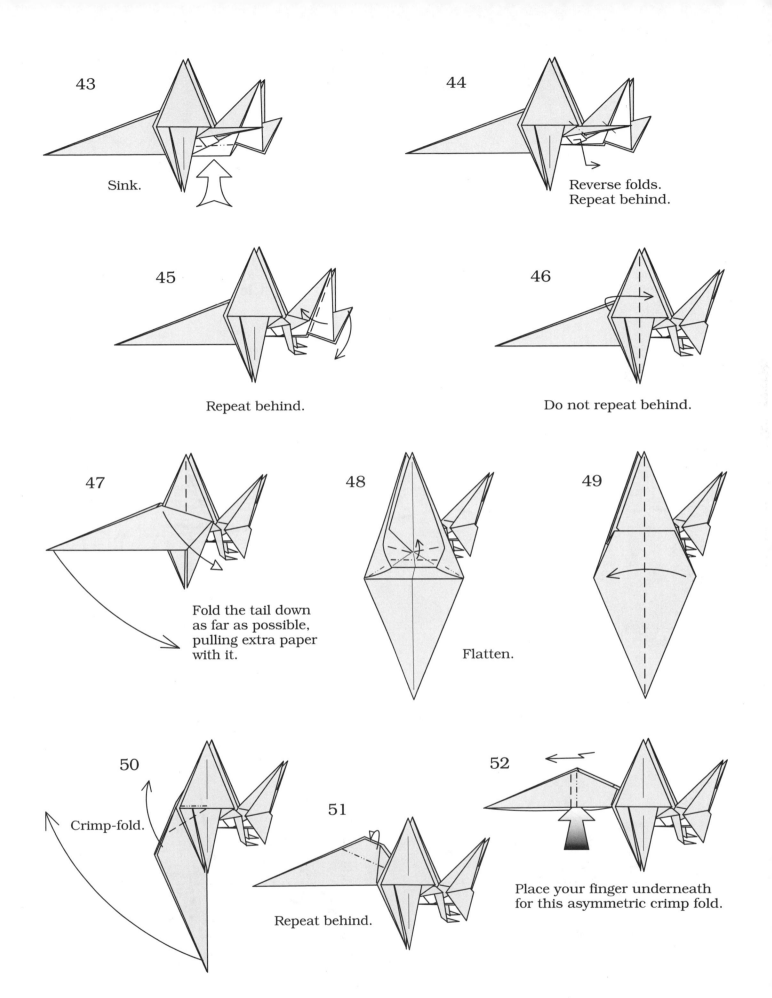

43

Sink.

44

Reverse folds.
Repeat behind.

45

Repeat behind.

46

Do not repeat behind.

47

Fold the tail down
as far as possible,
pulling extra paper
with it.

48

Flatten.

49

50

Crimp-fold.

51

Repeat behind.

52

Place your finger underneath
for this asymmetric crimp fold.

Wasp 95

53

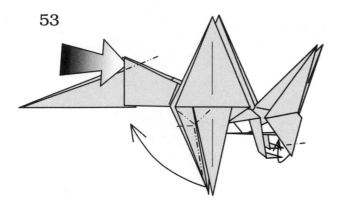

Reverse-fold at the tail and
head. Double-rabbit-ear the
legs. Repeat behind.

54

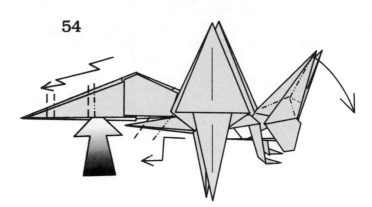

Double-rabbit-ear the antennae,
reverse-fold the legs, and
crimp-fold the tail. Repeat behind.

55

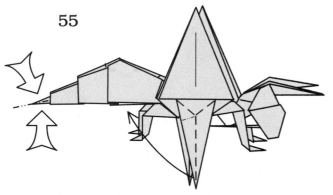

Squeeze the stinger and rabbit-ear
the legs. Repeat behind.

56

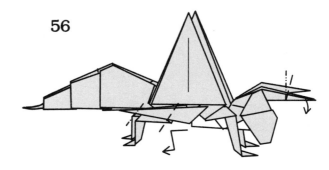

Outside-reverse-fold the legs
and crimp-fold the antennae.
Repeat behind.

57

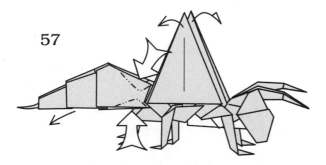

Shape the abdomen
and spread the wings.

58

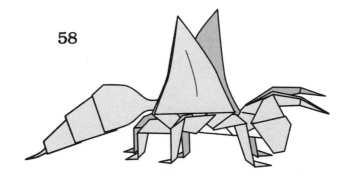

Wasp

Long-Horned Beetle

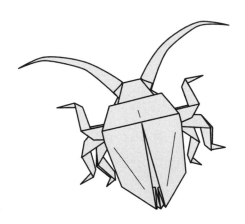

The Long-horned Beetle is one of the most destructive plant pests in the world. This pest has caused much devastation to countries throughout Asia and elsewhere around the world. At 1 1/4 inches long, this insect is coal black with irregular white spots on its back. The females chew notches in the bark of trees and deposit their eggs there. After the beetles mature, they burrow out of the tree in late Spring or Summer leaving small holes in the trees. Adult beetles feed on the leaves and bark of trees. The infested trees can be identified by either the beetles, the holes from the egg laying, sawdust around the trees, or by sap dripping from the trees.

1

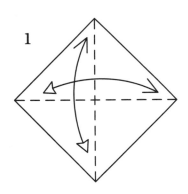

Fold and unfold.

2

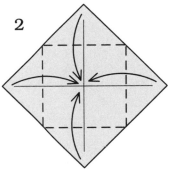

Blintz-fold.

3

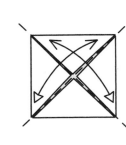

Fold and unfold.

4

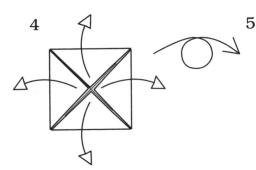

Unfold.

5

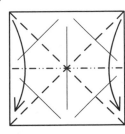

Make the
waterbomb base.

6

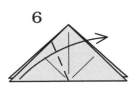

7

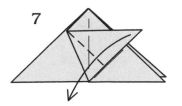

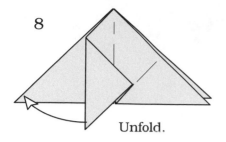

8

Unfold.

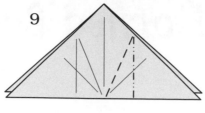

9

Repeat steps 6–8
on the right.

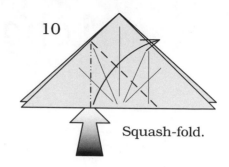

10

Squash-fold.

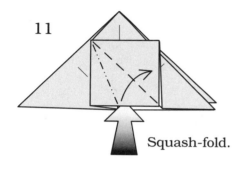

11

Squash-fold.

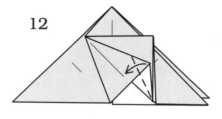

12

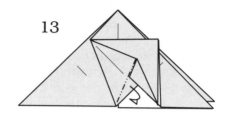

13

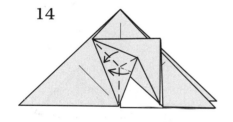

14

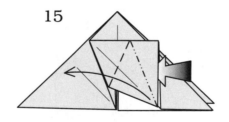

15

Squash-fold.

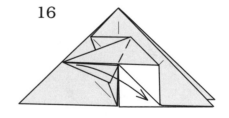

16

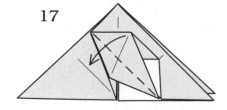

17

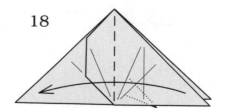

18

Fold the outer layer to the
left while keeping the
inner flap at the right.

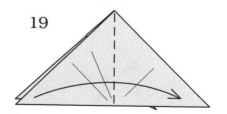

19

20

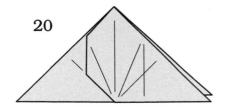

Repeat steps 10–17 on the right.

21

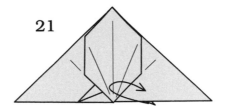

Pull out the flap.

22

Fold and unfold.

23

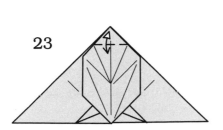

Fold and unfold.

24

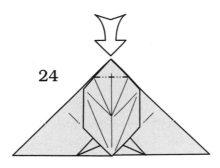

Sink.

25

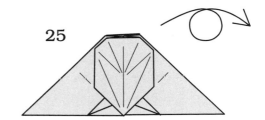

26

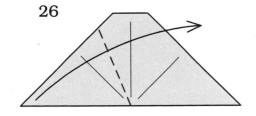

27

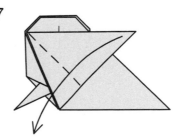

28

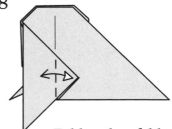

Fold and unfold.

29

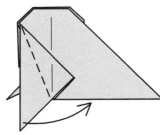

30

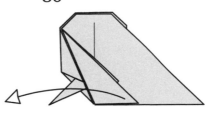

Unfold.

31

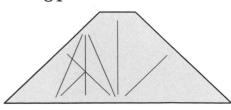

Repeat steps 26–30 on the right.

Long-Horned Beetle 99

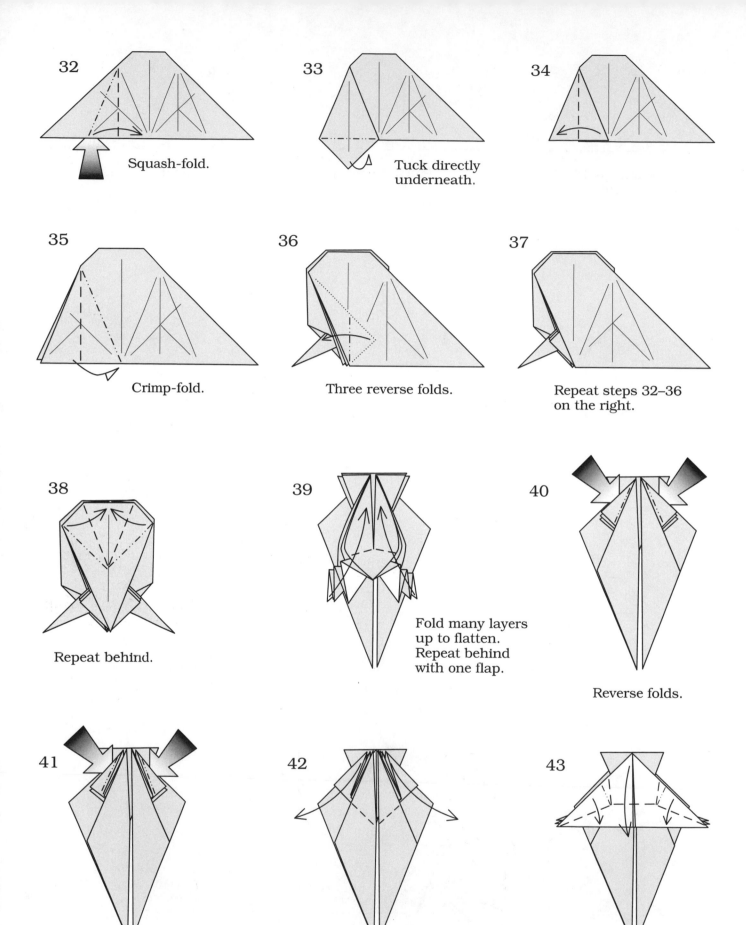

32 Squash-fold.

33 Tuck directly underneath.

34

35 Crimp-fold.

36 Three reverse folds.

37 Repeat steps 32–36 on the right.

38 Repeat behind.

39 Fold many layers up to flatten. Repeat behind with one flap.

40 Reverse folds.

41 Reverse folds.

42

43

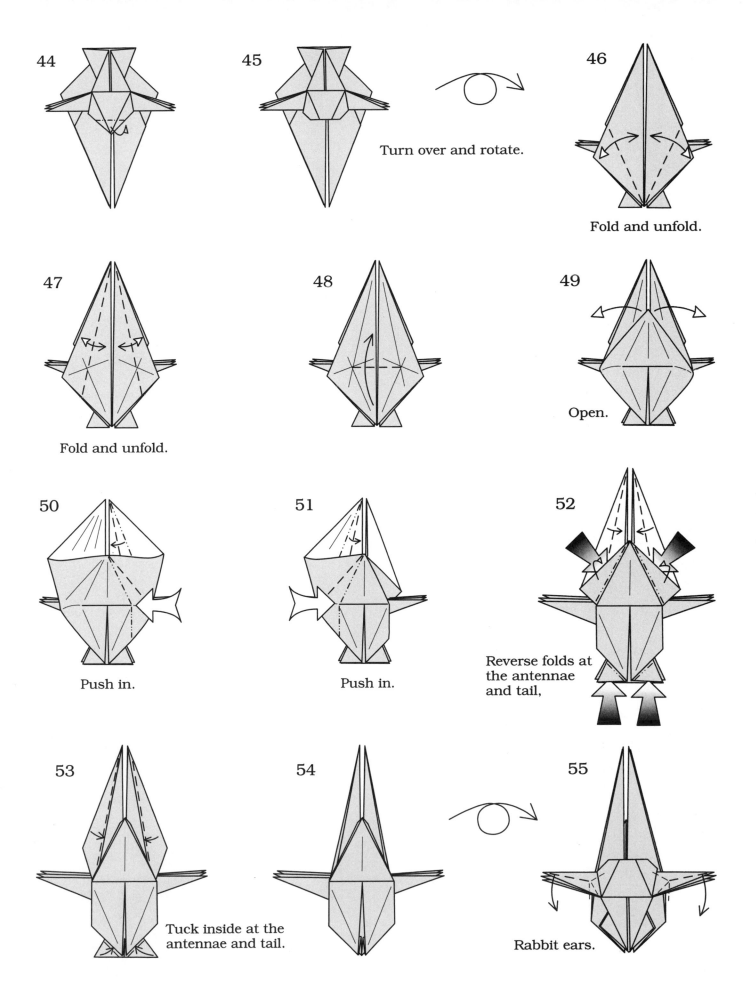

44

45

Turn over and rotate.

46

Fold and unfold.

47

Fold and unfold.

48

49

Open.

50

Push in.

51

Push in.

52

Reverse folds at the antennae and tail,

53

Tuck inside at the antennae and tail.

54

55

Rabbit ears.

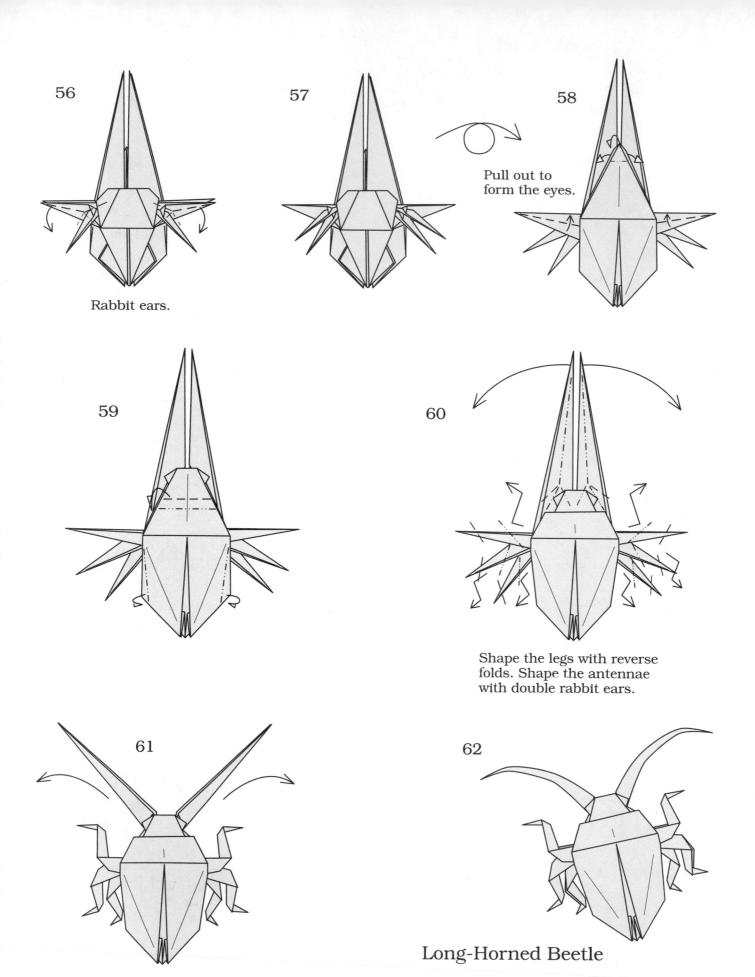

56

57

58

Pull out to form the eyes.

Rabbit ears.

59

60

Shape the legs with reverse folds. Shape the antennae with double rabbit ears.

61

62

Long-Horned Beetle

Earwig

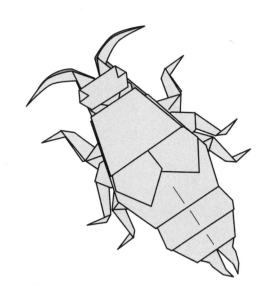

Earwigs are small insects that have large membranous hindwings that lie hidden under short, leathery forewings. The earwig varies from 5 to 50 millimeters in length and is flat, slender, and dark colored. This nocturnal insect is usually herbivorous. Several species can fire a foul-smelling liquid for distances up to 10 centimeters.

1

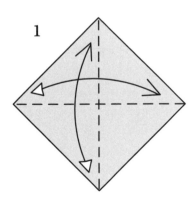

Fold and unfold.

2

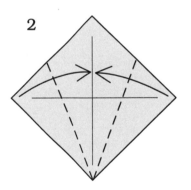

Kite-fold.

3

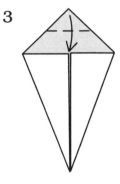

4

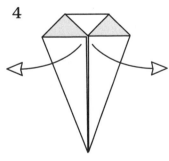

Unfold.

5

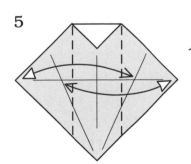

Fold and unfold.

6

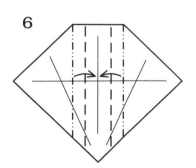

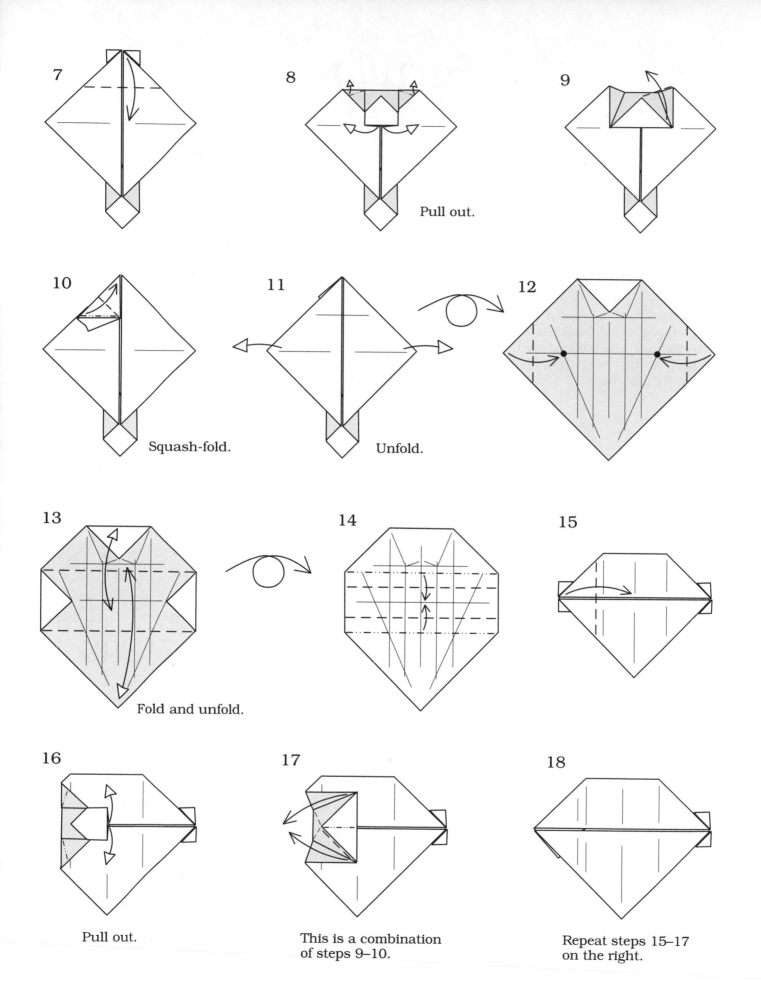

7

8

Pull out.

9

10

Squash-fold.

11

Unfold.

12

13

Fold and unfold.

14

15

16

Pull out.

17

This is a combination
of steps 9–10.

18

Repeat steps 15–17
on the right.

19

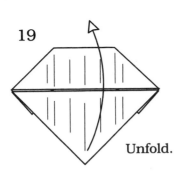

Unfold.

20

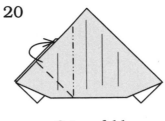

Crimp-fold.

21

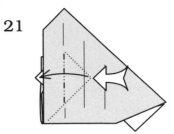

Reverse-fold.
Repeat behind.

22

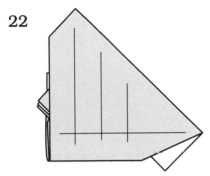

Repeat steps 20–21
on the right.

23

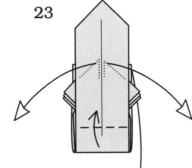

Fold up near the bottom,
on the crease. While doing
this, fold the layers from
behind down and pull out
the layers from inside to
the left and right.

24

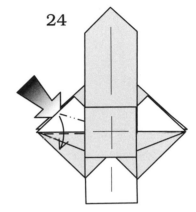

Squash-fold.

25

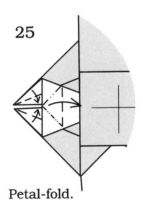

Petal-fold.

26

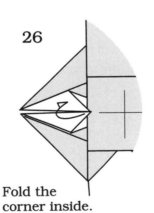

Fold the
corner inside.

27

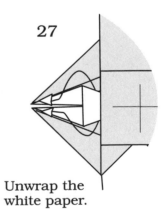

Unwrap the
white paper.

28

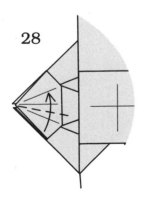

29

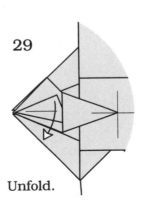

Unfold.

30

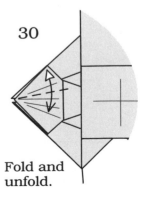

Fold and
unfold.

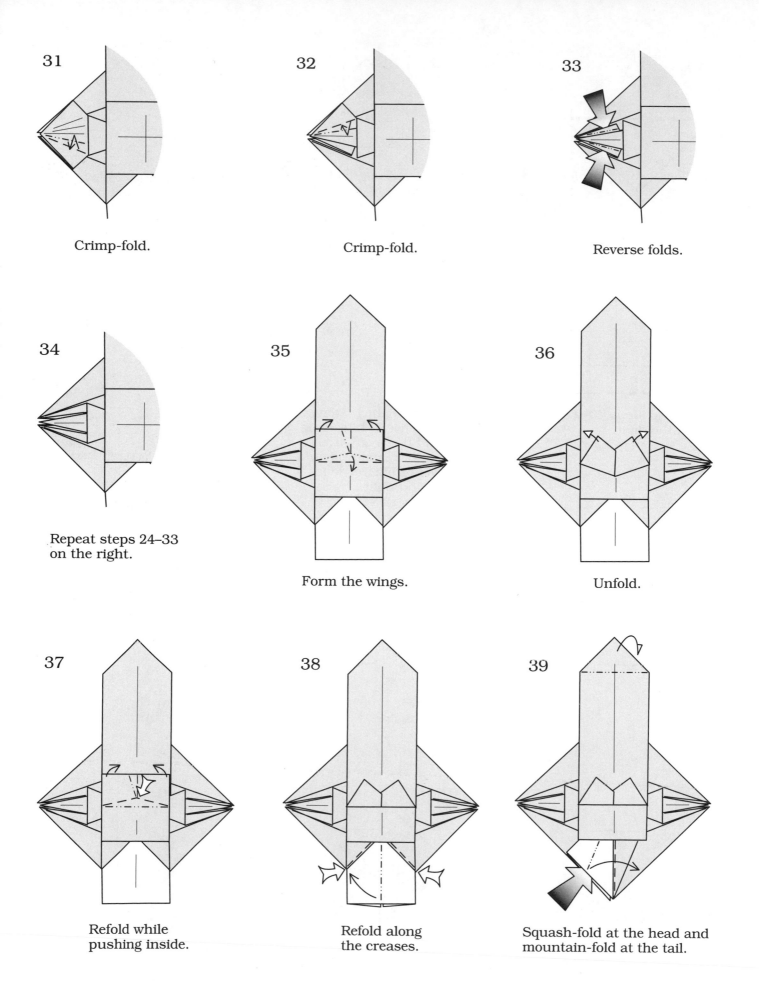

31

Crimp-fold.

32

Crimp-fold.

33

Reverse folds.

34

Repeat steps 24–33 on the right.

35

Form the wings.

36

Unfold.

37

Refold while pushing inside.

38

Refold along the creases.

39

Squash-fold at the head and mountain-fold at the tail.

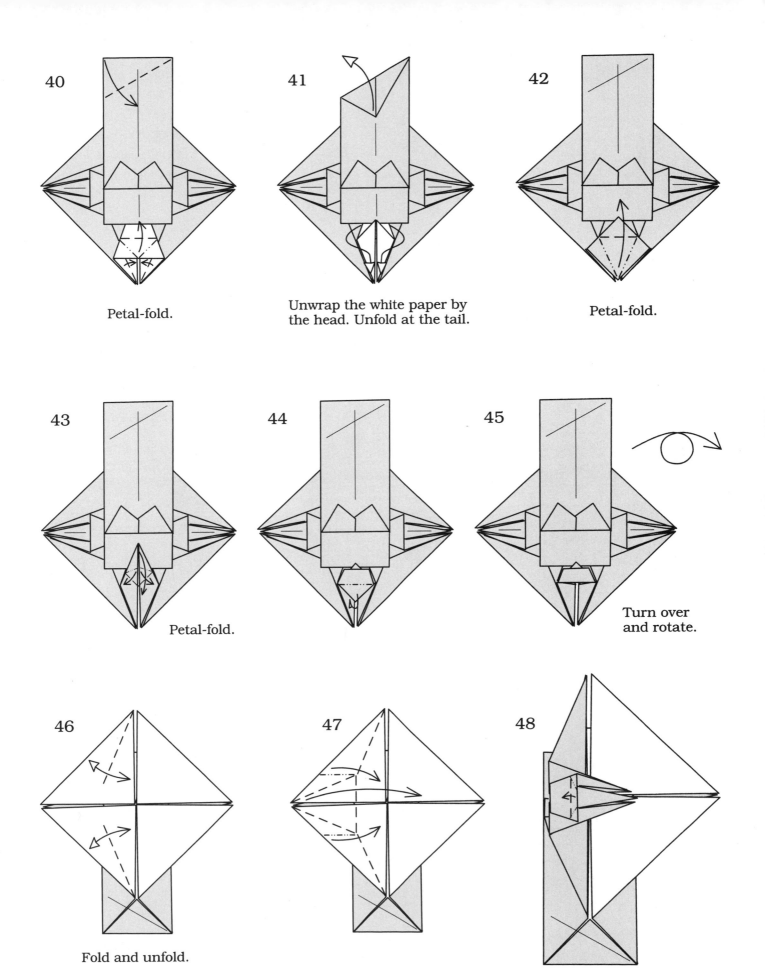

40

Petal-fold.

41

Unwrap the white paper by
the head. Unfold at the tail.

42

Petal-fold.

43

44

Petal-fold.

45

Turn over
and rotate.

46

Fold and unfold.

47

48

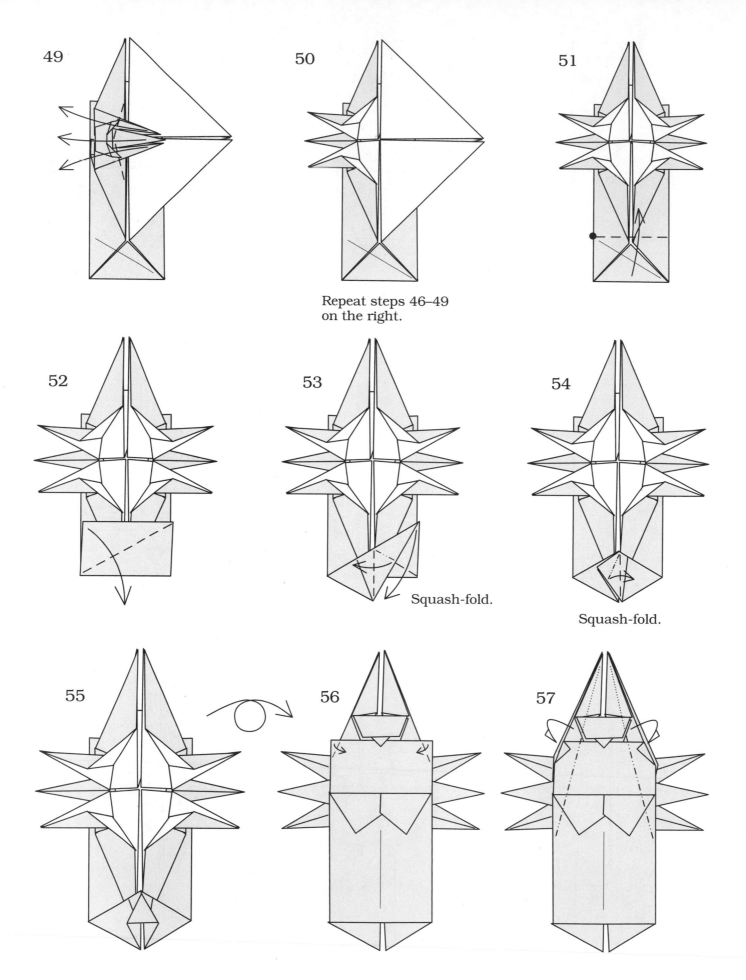

49

50

Repeat steps 46–49
on the right.

51

52

53

Squash-fold.

54

Squash-fold.

55

56

57

58

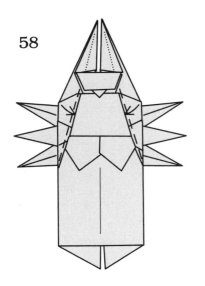

59

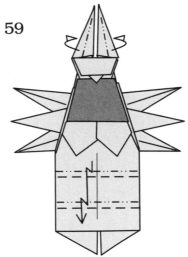

Fold both layers together
at the antennae.

60

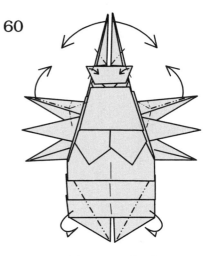

Rabbit-ear the legs
and reverse-fold
the antennae.

61

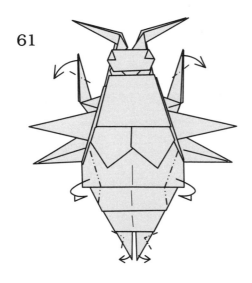

62

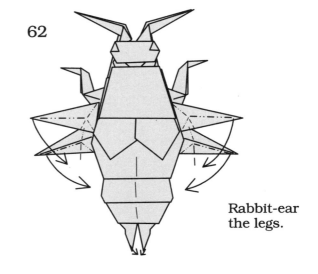

Rabbit-ear
the legs.

63

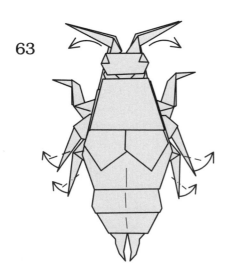

64

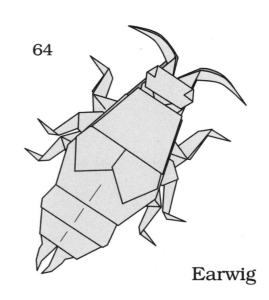

Earwig

Butterfly

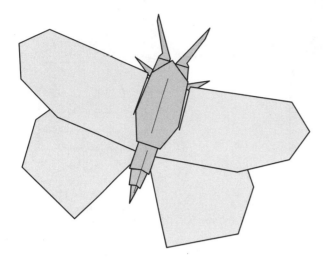

Butterflies are very colorful insects with four large wings. These wings are covered with tiny scales. Butterflies have a slender body and slender antennae. Many of the caterpillars we see are actually butterflies in their larval stage.

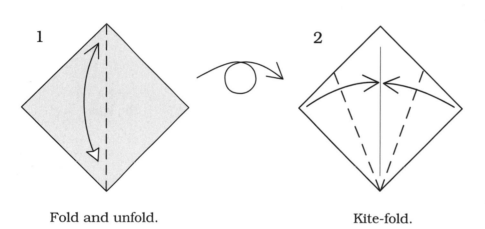

1

Fold and unfold.

2

Kite-fold.

3

Unfold.

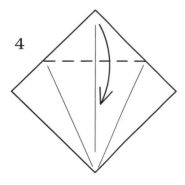

4

5

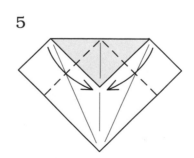

6

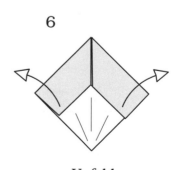

Unfold.

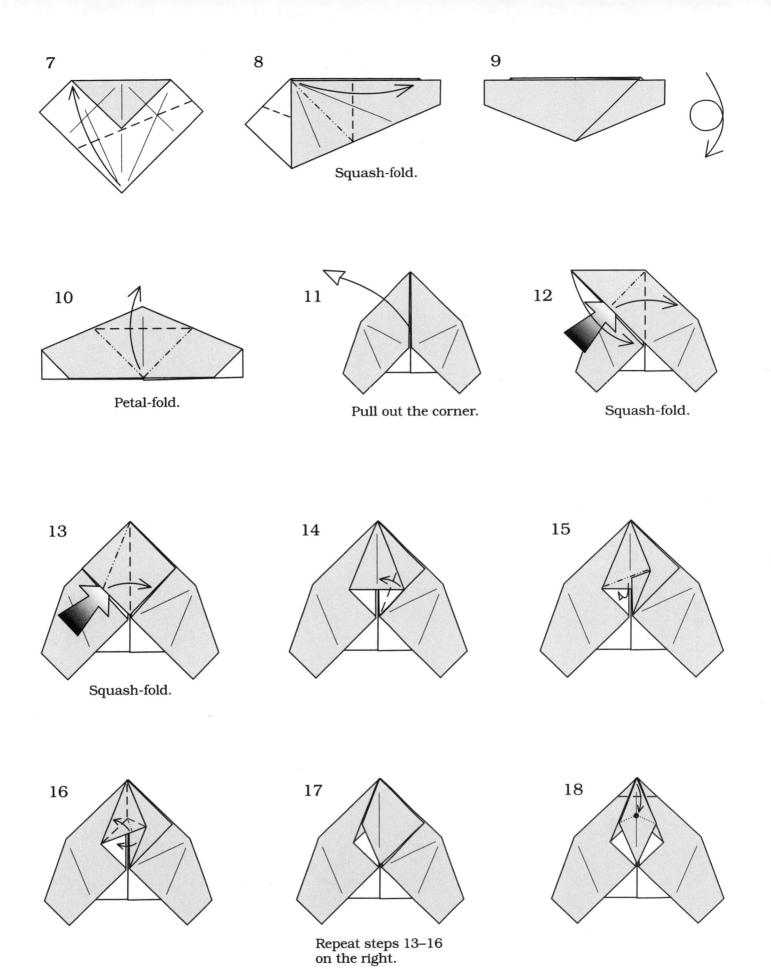

7

8

Squash-fold.

9

10

Petal-fold.

11

Pull out the corner.

12

Squash-fold.

13

Squash-fold.

14

15

16

17

Repeat steps 13–16
on the right.

18

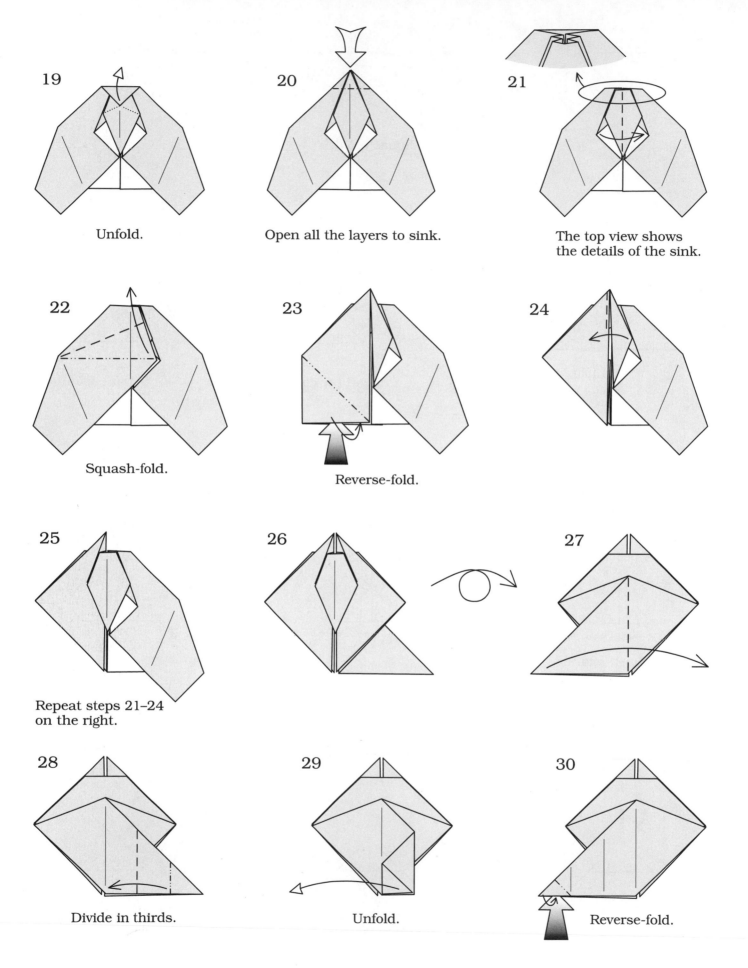

19 Unfold.

20 Open all the layers to sink.

21 The top view shows the details of the sink.

22 Squash-fold.

23 Reverse-fold.

24

25 Repeat steps 21–24 on the right.

26

27

28 Divide in thirds.

29 Unfold.

30 Reverse-fold.

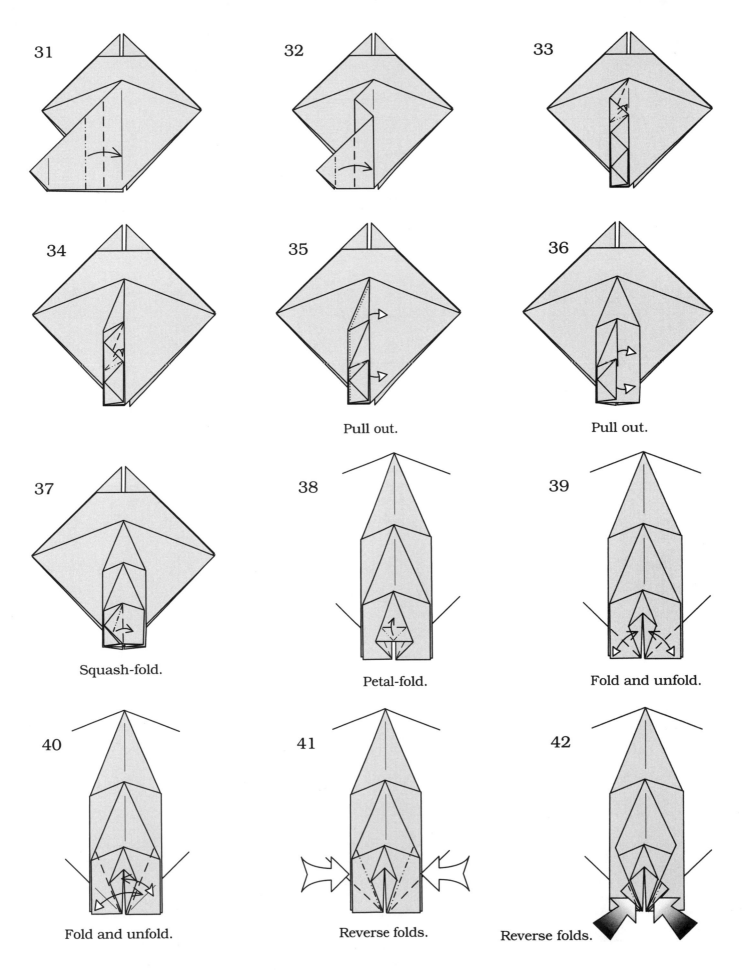

31

32

33

34

35

Pull out.

36

Pull out.

37

Squash-fold.

38

Petal-fold.

39

Fold and unfold.

40

Fold and unfold.

41

Reverse folds.

42

Reverse folds.

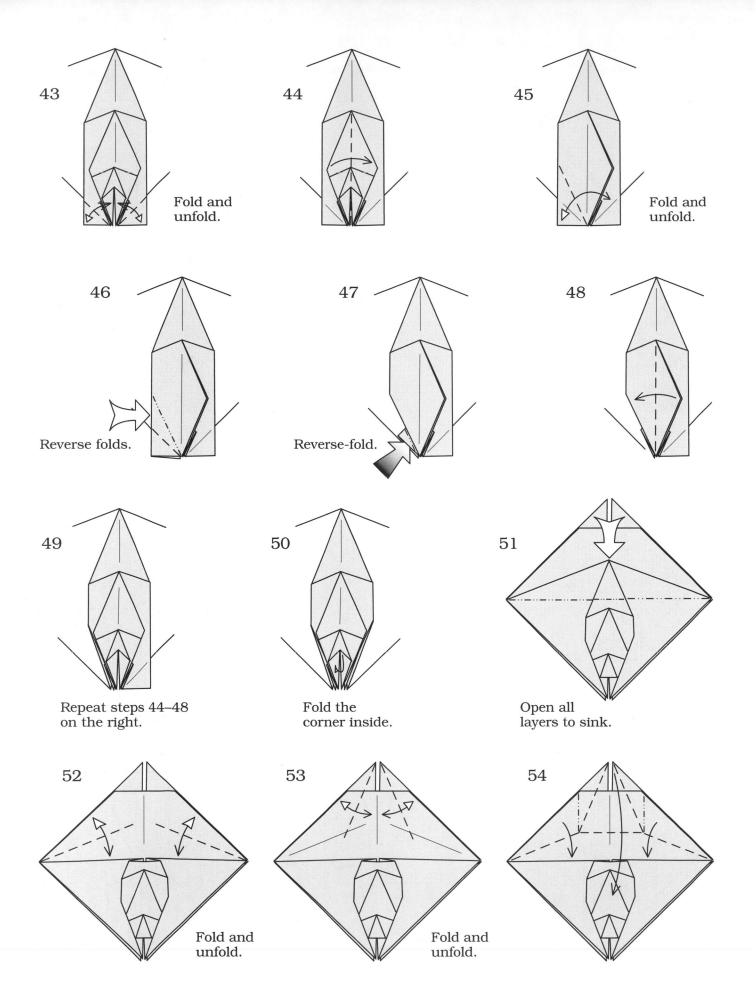

43 Fold and unfold.

44

45 Fold and unfold.

46 Reverse folds.

47 Reverse-fold.

48

49 Repeat steps 44–48 on the right.

50 Fold the corner inside.

51 Open all layers to sink.

52 Fold and unfold.

53 Fold and unfold.

54

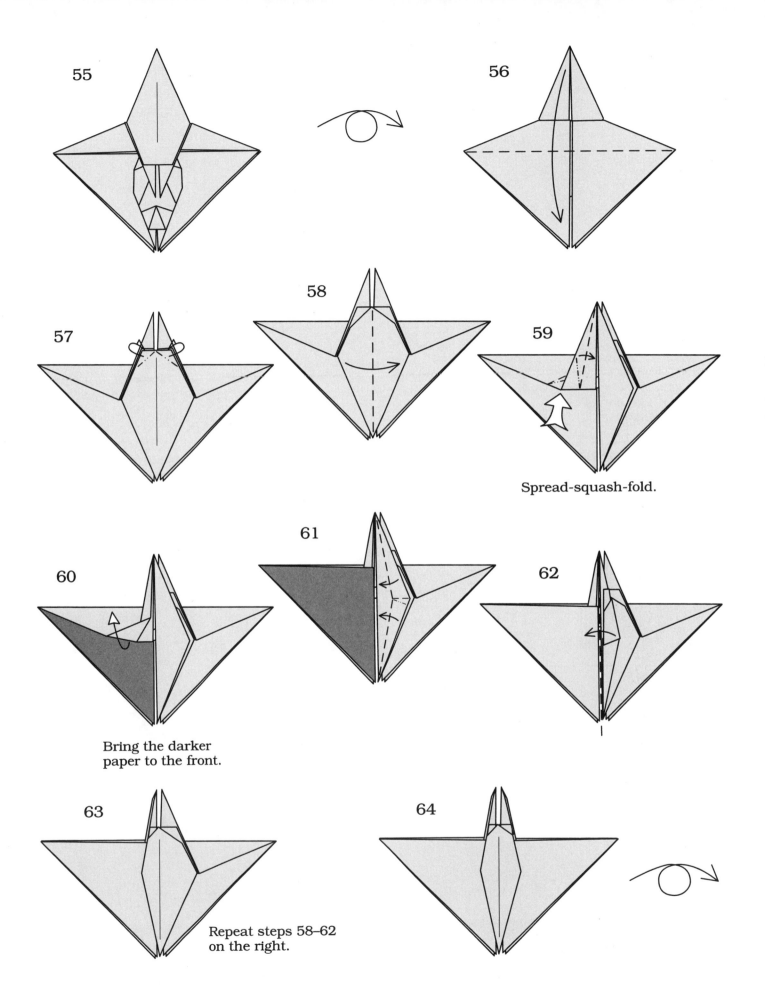

55

56

57

58

59

Spread-squash-fold.

60

Bring the darker
paper to the front.

61

62

63

Repeat steps 58–62
on the right.

64

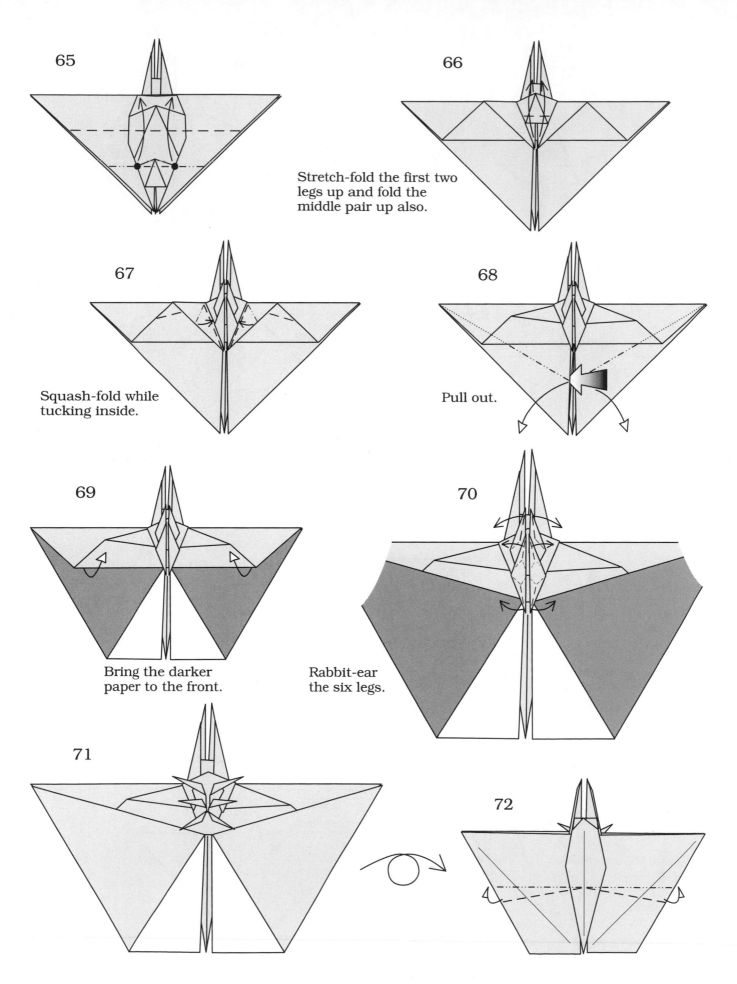

65

66

Stretch-fold the first two
legs up and fold the
middle pair up also.

67

Squash-fold while
tucking inside.

68

Pull out.

69

Bring the darker
paper to the front.

70

Rabbit-ear
the six legs.

71

72

73

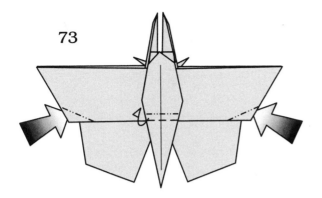

Reverse-fold the wings.

74

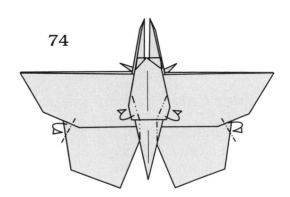

75

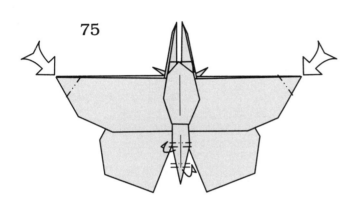

Sink the wing tips.

76

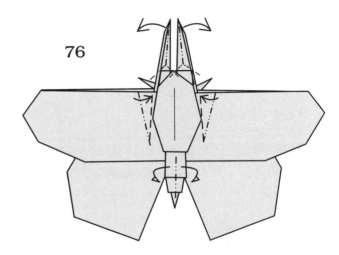

Thin the antennae. Bend the
tail. Lift the wings up slightly.

77

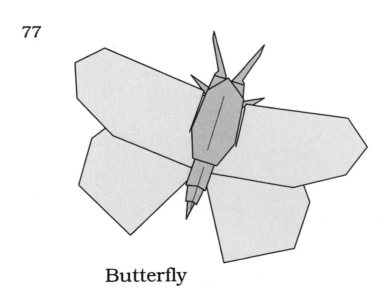

Butterfly

Basic Folds

Rabbit Ear.

To fold a rabbit ear, one corner is folded in half and laid down to a side.

1

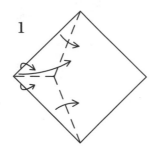

Fold a rabbit ear.

2

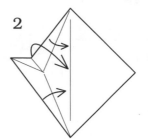

A three-dimensional intermediate step.

3

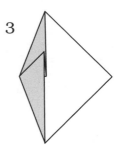

Double Rabbit Ear.

If you were to bend a straw you would be folding the double rabbit ear.

1

2

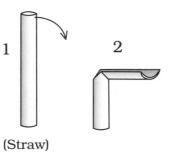

(Straw)

1

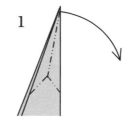

2

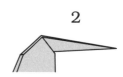

Make a double rabbit ear.

Squash Fold.

In a squash fold, some paper is opened and then made flat. The shaded arrow shows where to place your finger.

1

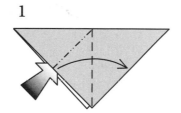

Squash-fold.

2

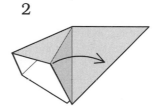

A three-dimensional intermediate step.

3

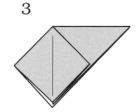

Petal Fold.

In a petal fold, one point is folded up while two opposite sides meet each other.

1

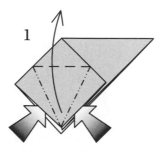

Petal-fold.

2

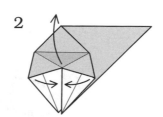

A three-dimensional intermediate step.

3

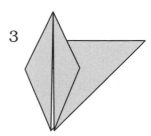

Inside Reverse Fold.

In an inside reverse fold, some paper is folded between layers. Here are two examples.

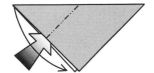

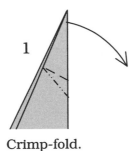

Reverse-fold.

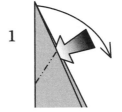

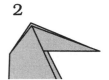

Reverse-fold.

Outside Reverse Fold.

Much of the paper must be unfolded to make an outside reverse fold.

Outside-reverse-fold.

Crimp Fold.

A crimp fold is a combination of two reverse folds.

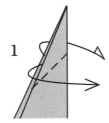

Crimp-fold.

Sink Fold.

In a sink fold, some of the paper without edges is folded inside. To do this fold, much of the model must be unfolded.

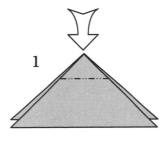

Sink.

Spread Squash Fold.

A cross between a squash fold and sink fold, some paper in the center is spread apart and then made flat.

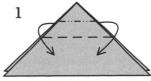

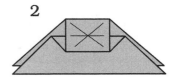

Spread-squash-fold.